SACKED!

What to Do When You Lose Your Job

Other books by Dean B. Peskin

The Corporate Casino (1978)
The Doomsday Job (1973)
Human Behavior and Employment Interviewing (1971)
The Building Blocks of EEO (1971)
The Art of Job Hunting (1967)

SACKED!

What to Do When You Lose Your Job

Dean B. Peskin

A DIVISION OF AMERICAN MANAGEMENT ASSOCIATIONS

Library of Congress Cataloging in Publication Data

Peskin, Dean B
    Sacked!

    Includes index.
    1. Applications for positions.   2. Employment
interviewing.   I. Title.
HF5383.P46   650'.14   79-13522
ISBN 0-8144-5547-6

First Printing

**To
Marcia, Debbie, and Cathy**

Preface

You lost your job!

Last year, according to the U.S. Department of Labor, over 12 million Americans lost their jobs too. From 10 to 12 million people lose their jobs every year in this country. If that doesn't give you much consolation, maybe it should. Most people survive the ordeal. You will too. It won't be easy, of course. Worthwhile achievements—reentering the workforce, rebuilding your confidence, and reaching toward new job achievements or your next career venture—never come easily. But you already know that.

O.K., you've lost your job. Now, what's the first thing you do? Panic, of course. It's an honest, up-front emotion. Nothing to be ashamed of. It's perfectly natural. It means that you are sincere and interested, involved in your own life and future. You are concerned about debts, your family, your self-esteem. Good traits.

Everyone panics at first. It's a natural reaction to a sudden, shocking, unexpected event. You're suddenly without a job, without alternatives. You're not sure which way to turn. It's confusing. You're faced with unfamiliar circumstances. That sets up physical reactions. Your heartbeat increases; so does your pulse. Your face gets flushed. You have trouble catching your breath. You eat too much or cannot eat at all. You have a feeling of impending disaster. You want to hide, avoid contact with other people. You lose interest in sex, lose sleep, lose your sense of humor. It goes away.

There is nothing wrong with panic, provided of course that you get over the panic stage and move into the planning stage. The major theme of this book is: Don't panic; plan.

Obviously, no responsible person plans to be without a major source of income. Suddenly without a job, you're in a footrace: your savings account (if you have one) against the calendar. The burning question becomes: Can you find a means of financial support before your money runs out? Another burning question is: Can you find emotional relief before your nerves give out? We'll see. Now is the time when the worries and upsets start to pile up. What we can do together in this book is put an invisible bandage on the worries and ease the pain.

It's painful to face potential financial disaster, emotional disorientation, and career collapse. It takes an absolute fool to face this with a stiff upper lip. But notice I said *potential* disaster. There's nothing certain about it. Still, you must deal with the facts. You can't rip out your swimming pool and give it back just because you can no longer afford the payments. You can't tell the orthodontist that your kids' teeth can wait until next year. You can't tell your stomach to stop feeling hungry. You can't tell the landlord he doesn't really need your rent. And you can't suddenly decide to become a beach bum when your emotional and psychological makeup won't buy it.

Your first thoughts are directed toward the very basics of life—the fundamentals, the "back to nature" needs. When you had a job, paid your bills, saved a little when you could, felt sort of successful and fulfilled, you could afford to worry about things like whether people like you and admire you, and you could concern yourself with where your next self-actualizing experience was coming from. But now it's different. You're worrying about the basics: career, bills, and emotional stability. Whether you know it or not, you've just learned a little about Abraham Maslow's complex theory on the hierarchy of human needs. So remember that it's natural to think about the essentials of life. That isn't panic; it's good thinking.

At such times people get what I like to call the stereophonic blahs. Depressing worries come from all sides. How long will I be out of work? Will my money hold out until I find something? Will my wife or husband stop loving me? Will my wife or husband *start* loving me? Do creditors really repossess things? What will my kids think now that I seem to have less of a future than they have? What will my friends think? How do I overcome the simple embarrassment of this mess? What effect will losing my job have on a prospective employer? Is this the time to change careers or go back to school?

These questions are difficult to answer. But I'll tell you what *we will do together.* We'll probe the problem of rebuilding personal confidence and pride. We'll explore alternative ways of solving your problems. We'll discover a plan of action that works best for you. My role will be to sort out the various opportunities that are available to you, to sort through the tangled mess of fears and anxieties and discover some avenues of escape that are positive and productive. I will suggest ways of dealing with these problems and opportunities. Then we'll tie together the whole thing into a workable strategy. A few chapters from now, to make sure you're on the right track, I'll give you some ways of making certain you aren't unknowingly playing tricks on yourself. This is sometimes called subconscious withdrawal. It can hurt you in the job market when you reenter later on.

Now, that's what I'm going to do. *Your* role will be to keep an open mind and take a fresh, new look at things. Feel free at any time to shout back at my suggestions and remarks.

Let's talk about what planning means. Our goal is to evolve a workable rebuilding strategy for the future. Planning is really very simple. It is imagining what we would like to see happen in the future and then devising ways to make it happen. Simple enough? It can be a lot of fun if you let your mind go free and gradually admit to your needs and desires. You can't always do that right away; it may take a while.

I remember counseling a young man who expressed an interest in a career in financial management. We developed a plan of action and a strategy and spent considerable time talking about the commitment he would have to make. Then, when we were ready to tie the whole thing into an action plan with target dates and reevaluation checkpoints, he said to me, "My mother will be very happy." His mother! What about *him?* You see, it was not until he involved himself in a realistic plan that he was moved toward escaping from it. As long as his goal was abstract, somewhere off in the future and ill defined, he could accept it. But once he dealt with the reality of it and visualized himself working through the plan, he felt trapped. Only then was he willing and emotionally ready to confront his hidden career desire.

The truth is losing your job can be a blessing in disguise. It forces you into the kind of self-appraisal you didn't have time for when you started down the road to success. You couldn't bother with such things then. They held out little value. You *knew* that somehow you would make it. Many people have been saved from lifelong careers they disliked, from mental and physical and, yes, marital breakdowns because the loss of a job forced them to take a good, hard look at themselves.

There are few adult experiences that can change our lives so drastically and few that present us with so many opportunities to build for a stronger, more productive, and more satisfying future. Let's face it, there is nothing pleasant about losing your job. But once it happens you have to live with it, accept it, adjust to it, and then move yourself out of unemployment into some kind of productive effort, if making a productive effort is what you want. If it isn't, you've accomplished what you set out to do: be without work. You don't have to reenter the job market after being sacked. You can, of course, never return. It is up to you. And the decision to reenter the job market after experiencing a setback such as being sacked is one you must arrive at. When you do, the attitudes you carry into the job market are going to affect your success on the next job.

This is not a magic book. It doesn't contain mystical wisdom on how to overcome your weaknesses or secrets about where to find the perfect job. It is, however, a book of alternatives, of approaches, of new ways of seeing the same old problem—and yourself. I hope it is a book of challenges as well. My task, as I see it, is to present you with some alternative ways of thinking when you are sacked. Your task is to decide which alternatives are best for you. It's a burden I hope you will gladly share with me.

Dean B. Peskin

Contents

1

The Emotional Side
of Losing a Job

O.K. Feeling States

Losing your job is fraught with emotional peaks and valleys. You experience high anxiety and frustration, possibly even guilt. And that is good. Indeed, these feeling states have extraordinary value at a time like this. It's O.K. to feel these surges of emotion. The important part of your job-losing experience is to keep sight of this fact and be ready to live with it. You are going to experience anxiety, frustration, and guilt, and it is O.K.

Two things, however, you must do. First, understand the difference between anxiety and frustration and, second, understand why these are not harmful emotions when controlled.

Anxiety and frustration are related, but they are different in terms of the time intervals in which they manifest themselves. Here's what I mean. Frustration is an emotional reaction to very painful events that either have taken place in your life in the past or are taking place right now. Anxiety is future-oriented. It is an emotional reaction to future events or your apprehension about them. Here is a statement which combines both concepts: "Ye, gad! I lost my job. How will I pay the rent?"

Now let's talk a little about the difference between fear and anxiety. Let me explain it this way. The question "How will I pay the rent?" is an expression of anxiety in that it is general and helpless but does not state the specific fear which prompts the outcry. The fear is that you will be evicted. Fear is the recognition or identification of a specific danger. Anxiety is a general, somewhat diffuse apprehension about a painful experience which may happen.

Anxiety and Job Loss

Anxiety is perhaps the most overwhelming emotion people feel when they are sacked. Anxiety can be highly exhausting and destructive to your emotional and physical well-being. It tends to wear away at you, nagging and gnawing so persistently that there seems to be no escape. It takes hold in such a pervasive way that, like a dye in water, it discolors every facet of your thinking. There is a reason and it has nothing to do with your emotional stability, intelligence, character, or maturity—the factors usually blamed when people become "worrywarts."

The reason anxiety attacks when you get sacked is that your entire pattern of security is threatened. Anxiety attacks that intricate little network of security you have developed over the years, and when this network is threatened, the very foundation of your life becomes threatened. Fear doesn't work that way. Fear is specific, remember? We fear *because* of a pattern of security. Our pattern of security has taught us to fear those things which threaten our way of life. Likewise, we fear losing those things that we value and that are vulnerable or may be challenged.

When we've been sacked, the entire fortress we've built against life's contingencies is threatened. Where do we go? Nowhere, it seems, and that is why anxiety eats away in all directions; it's pulling the rug right out from under us. What is at the heart of this anxiety? Our values, which we consider absolutely essential to our existence and our survival. And because we can't quite put our finger on any one element of our security that is being threatened, the entire structure becomes threatened.

Anxiety which presents a total threat to our security pattern is too destructive and much too difficult to deal with over a long period of time. The subsequent victims of this destructiveness are our confidence, physical and emotional well-being, attitudes, and self-image, which affects our ability to reach for new career goals. This chain reaction is probably the most critical factor in rebuilding after the loss of a job.

Coping with Anxiety

There are two basic kinds of anxiety: normal and neurotic. Let's talk about the normal kind first. Yes, some anxiety is considered "normal." Normal anxiety, the apprehension rational people live with all the time, is a part of our lives. Feelings of anxiety may come and go, but we know that sooner or later they will be back. Now, if you are a normal, rational individual there are several ways you will deal with anxiety. First, you don't see the outcome (whatever it may be) of the threat as being wholly disproportionate to the threat itself. You may say, but not really believe the statement "If I lose my job, the world is going to come to an end." It won't, and the rational person knows it. The irrational person may believe it or consider it a possibility.

The second way in which rational, normal people deal with anxiety is by avoiding repression; that is, by refusing to shut out the distressful feelings which arouse guilt, anxiety, fear, and helplessness. Repression is a make-believe situation in many respects in that the individual chooses to "forget" or ignore the threatening situation. Thus an individual who *refuses to see* that unless new skills are learned or existing ones strengthened, the job hunt will soon be over is repressing the painfulness of such a realization. Rational people face up to the facts—the sources of their anxiety—and develop ways of coping with them.

Finally, in dealing with anxiety, rational, "together" people do not embrace various defense mechanisms. For example, they do not become paranoid and see their job loss as a grand conspiracy by those jealous or fearful of them. They do not become psychosomatically ill or consider suicide. Their panic is transient and disappears in short order. Freud called manageable anxiety "objective anxiety" in order to emphasize the point that it can be controlled in constructive ways and that destructive behavior can be avoided.

But it is true that neurotic anxiety can be observed frequently in organizations. People go into "tailspins" from which they seem incapable of extricating themselves. Consider the individual who has been demoted and within a relatively short time is sacked. He probably hasn't fully recovered from the effects of the demotion when he is hit with yet another anxiety-producing event. This is a classic case of neurotic anxiety: The individual's inability to cope with a previous anxiety-producing situation helps produce the next anxiety-provoking experience and may slow the individual's ability to work out feelings of anxiety and behave constructively.

This is the person who just can't snap out of it. He sulks, is depressed, is down on himself, feels sorry for himself, defeated. What happens? He begins to mess up on his new job and before you know it, he's out. And what do people tell him? Oh, they say things like "Grow up!" and "Get your act together!" These statements make about as much sense as telling a failing employee to do better. Such are the generalities that people feel called upon to utter, but they really don't help. In fact, they add to anxiety. The thing we have to do when we are sacked is consider the best ways to confront our anxiety.

Confronting Anxiety

A classic theorist in the field of behavioral science wrote in the late nineteenth century that anxiety is a great teacher; that people who have once faced anxiety and survived are better able to face anxiety in the future. Many modern behavioral scientists have supported his view. That's encouraging, isn't it? This may account for why young managers react to seemingly minor setbacks with powerful emotions and why the "old pro" tends to be a bit more restrained. Of course, personality plays a part, as do values. But on balance, once we have survived an anxiety-ridden period, the more optimistic we tend to be about the outcome of the next anxiety-producing episode in our lives. We learn to confront the anxiety and we find that neurotic reactions just aren't our style.

In order to deal constructively with our anxiety at being sacked, we must begin to define it and cut it down to size. We must become specific about the threat we feel and rational about the outcome. We can begin to cope by focusing on specifics. For example, we should ask ourselves:

1. Will my creditors give me more time?
2. Will my savings hold out?
3. What sacrifices will my family endure? What do they understand about my present situation?
4. In what ways will a long period of unemployment hurt my chances of getting a good job?
5. What interim jobs can I get to ease the burden while I am looking for the job I want?

6. Is it my pride or my pocketbook that drives me toward panic-related decisions?

Questions such as these help us to reduce anxiety, to define the nature and extent of the threat. Once our specific fears are pinpointed, we can begin to relieve ourselves of that pervasive feeling of doom which attacks our entire pattern of security.

High Anxiety, Low Anxiety

Are you a high-anxiety or low-anxiety person? Which one you are will have an important effect on how you deal with job loss and reentry into the job market. Being one or the other type is neither necessarily good nor bad; each is different and each carries with it different behaviors in relation to success and failure. Success seekers, those who willingly set very high achievement goals and who strive for success at high aspiration levels, usually are low-anxiety people, particularly in work situations where their performance is under continual evaluation by those in authority. These are the people who, when feeling threatened in some way, seem to perform so well.

The individual who seeks to avoid failure is a high-anxiety person. This is the fellow who takes few if any risks; he plays it close to the vest. He is not nearly as interested in achievement as he is in avoiding failure. These people are anxiety-prone in work situations, particularly when they know that the focus of attention is on them. Their anxiety simply gets in the way of their performance and their most anxious thoughts often seem to be reinforced when they do not succeed.

But here is some good news for both types of people. High-anxiety failure avoiders usually do an excellent job when emphasis is placed on the task at hand, on what is to be done, and not on their ability to perform the task.

When they do not feel threatened, they actually perform better than the achievement-oriented person with lofty aspirations who does not feel threatened. High-anxiety people are not looking for challenges; they simply want a task to perform, without risk, without putting themselves and their reputations on the line. High-anxiety people tend to see almost every situation as a test of themselves, their character, endurance, dedication, skills—whatever it is that concerns them.

This is very significant in terms of being sacked and preparing for the comeback. If you are a high-anxiety type, you can view the coming-back process as a series of steps in rebuilding and reevaluating your perspective, your skills, and your career objectives. View it as a set of clearly defined tasks which represent a logical progression from the point of being sacked to the assumption of job responsibilities once again. You've been employed and you've functioned in a productive manner; you will again through a series of tasks which can be performed with some thought, self-appraisal, and planning. The low-anxiety person can view the loss of a job and the rebuilding process as a challenge to his motivation, dedication, ability, character, and self-esteem. The entire process threatens his self-concept, his self-worth. This is intolerable, for it creates a barrier in his struggle to achieve, to prove his worth to himself and others. It's a personal matter. He begins to look within for the strength and courage to go on.

Anxiety as a Motivator

Anxiety in moderate amounts motivates or spurs on the individual. Anxiety over a long period of time can be crushing and produce debilitated, dysfunctional people who fall back on rigid, unproductive habits. These patterns have a great deal to do with our ability to respond constructively to being sacked. Following the first blush of shock and panic, people often experience a surge of motivation and energy. They scurry off to read the want ads, write their resume, visit employment agencies and search firms, renew old acquaintances who can be of help, and take constructive, often creative and optimistic approaches toward rebuilding their confidence and reentering the job market.

If, however, joblessness persists over a long period of time, anxiety mounts. Savings begin to dwindle and worries about the basic needs of food and shelter mount. People fall back on old habits and unproductive solutions. They become less creative and adaptive, and more pessimistic.

In such a situation, the individual who typically takes great pains to solve problems is likely to jump at the first offer that will help relieve the pressure of anxiety. He may even disregard obvious clues about the instability of the company. During the early stages of anxiety, these clues would have been identified and given deep consideration. Irritability, headaches, stomach cramps, nervousness, excessive smoking and drinking often appear at this stage. Unable to differentiate between good and bad employment opportunities in terms of his skills and career development to date, the sacked individual may send his resume to almost any company that seems to present an employment possibility. The individual seems to be in a race with time—no, usually in a race with his savings account or with the collateral he may need to borrow money so he can keep the roof over his head. The individual's performance as a job hunter and, even prior to that, as a problem solver and decision maker suffers.

Frustration and Job Loss

Frustration is another powerful emotion people experience when they are sacked. What could be more frustrating than the interruption of a job, a career, a savings program, and a lifestyle? Frustration is the stress we feel when an outside event blocks what we want.

Once again, in moderate doses, frustrating events prompt us to accelerate our drives and energies in an effort to either overcome the obstacle or maneuver around it. Sometimes our frustrations cause us to seek out secondary solutions which eventually prove to be as satisfying as primary solutions. For example, a secretary unable to find permanent work may decide to work for a temporary-help agency while looking for longer-range employment. She keeps her skills current, earns a living (perhaps not as much as she might otherwise but at least she is not destitute), and continues her job hunt. Managers sometimes become consultants; a few start their own firms. Some take any job in order to keep a roof over their heads and food on the table. Sometimes sacked individuals return to school to learn new skills and improve old ones.

But frustration also has its negative side. Often the frustration we feel about the setback in our lives spills over into other areas and affects our performance. For example, an individual who is sacked may suddenly become inattentive to a spouse or alienate friends by lapsing into long periods of silence and meditation, worry and concern. Hobbies which once attracted the individual are no longer interesting or exciting. Gardens go unattended and stamp collections lose their appeal. Sometimes the sacked person loses his sense of humor, and why not? It is difficult to be frivolous when you watch your bank account dwindle to zero or feel the scorn of friends and associates and possibly the disapproval of a mate.

Guilt—a Persistent Menace

Guilt is perhaps the most difficult of all feeling states we experience when we are sacked. It is a deadly inhibitor to clear thinking and constructive behavior. One of the main reasons guilt produces such negative effects is because we are never quite certain whether we really should feel guilty about being sacked and for how long. Also, we never know at what point our guilt is washed away. Because there are so many unknowns involved with guilt, it is difficult to mediate these feelings and rid ourselves of them.

Still, much like anxiety and frustration, guilt can act as a motivator, spurring us on to overcome our feelings and to emerge successful in reentering the job market. But too much guilt becomes harmful. Deep feelings of guilt can often lead to a total collapse of organized, rational behavior and in extreme conditions even drive the individual toward self-destruction. One manager I know who was sacked felt so guilty about his inability to provide for his wife and family that he became an alcoholic and nearly ruined his life.

Much of the guilt we feel on being sacked is induced by cultural influences. We live in a society in which winning, being number one, is everything. "You can do it," "You can win," "You can succeed" are drummed into our consciousness from early childhood with unrelenting persistence. It isn't good enough to be second or third or even to have tried; being number one is what counts. And the materialistic aspects of our society support that early teaching.

But do people really have to feel so guilty when they lose their jobs? I doubt it. You may have given the job your best shot and it wasn't appreciated. Perhaps a personality conflict contributed to your being sacked, or perhaps an economic downturn created a financial crisis for the company. Certainly these circumstances cannot even remotely be considered a breach of conduct on your part. If you goofed up on the job and you know it was squarely your fault, then you must take responsibility. But do not let the guilt you feel overpower you. Knowing how you messed up and why is satisfactory penance. Learn from your mistake and do better next time.

Above all, don't confuse guilt with disappointment. You can feel deep disappointment about not being able to afford that vacation to Hawaii or that luxurious car you promised your wife or the savings account you hoped to build by Christmas. That's disappointment—not realizing a fond hope or expectation. But it is not the same thing as guilt over a breach of conduct or behavior. Your emotional health and your ability to recover from the setback of having been fired may hang in the balance.

Learning from Failure

If I all but assure you that you can and will successfully complete a given project and even suggest that doing so will gain you the adulation of others, then I have given you a mental set that influences your actions. You clearly expect to win, to achieve, to receive praise and admiration. You are prepared for the role of being number one. Now, let us assume that you finish the project and I say, "Terrible! You've failed! You're a washout! Get out of here!" You're going to be disappointed, disoriented, and thoroughly frustrated and anxiety-ridden. Why? Because you never once were told that you might fail. You weren't prepared for it. Your mental set was directed toward winning and the defeat was crushing.

Now, suppose I told you before you began the project that, indeed, there was the possibility of failure, and then you failed as I told you you might. How do you feel? Well, you probably feel disappointed, maybe a little crushed, if you really wanted to succeed in the project. But your disappointment was minimized by my suggestion that failure was possible. The point here is that your expectations about future events have a great deal to do with your ability to deal with the emotional trauma of being sacked.

People who do not blindly believe that their employment situation will never change are able to cope with unemployment rationally. Employees in high-turnover industries such as electronics usually experience very little trauma when they lose their jobs. Employees in more stable industries take job loss much harder. They tend to blame themselves rather than "other causes" and have a more difficult time coming to terms with being sacked. Unprepared for the possibility of failure, they do not develop the mental set necessary to deal with it.

Anticipating failure on the job and thus the possibility of job loss can spur individuals to develop a plan of action in case such events occur. People may, for example, prepare a resume and begin to survey the job market for possible alternatives. Such preparedness can help them avoid an unrealistic sense of job security and reduce the trauma associated with being sacked.

Expectations about success and failure are critically important when it comes to choosing a company and even an occupation. As an executive recruiter for many years, I found that young, upwardly mobile executives who had experienced some degree of success rarely verbalized the possibility of failure in their future career. Now we know that failure is usually a forbidden topic in interviews. Applicants are not expected to even consider the possibility and certainly not to verbalize it.

When I interviewed managerial candidates for jobs, I usually asked them what they would do if they failed to achieve a particularly important goal as a manager. Most went into incredible detail about how they would go about achieving the goal and few if any could give me a well-thought-out description of what they might do in the face of failure. One young candidate for a mangerial job said, "But I won't fail. I won't." "But what if you do?" I insisted. He replied, "But I won't." While his enthusiasm and confidence were impressive, his lack of maturity, experience, and almost adolescent certainty about the future disturbed me.

The more experienced executive who has won a few and lost a few, *as we all do,* typically will answer the question with one of the following: "I'll analyze why I failed." "I'll try to understand what caused me to fail and then next time try to avoid those circumstances that brought about the failure." "I'll get away from the project for a while, then with fresh perspective I'll try it again." "I'll try to understand what I did wrong." "I'll figure out how much of the failure was my fault, the result of bad timing, or somebody else's fault, and then attack the weak spot next time." These are constructive approaches to failure. They are the responses of people who have failed, have learned from their failures, and have learned to consider the possibility of failure in the future.

Responses to Being Sacked

As we look at the matter of job loss and seek ways to rebuild our confidence and begin to behave constructively and rationally, we must explore how the reasons for our job loss can affect our ability to continue striving toward career objectives. Let me give you two examples.

We'll begin with the individual who is called into his boss's office and told that he is sacked. Why? Well, the boss doesn't like him. He doesn't like his easygoing attitude in the face of the company's obvious problems, his willingness to take off on Saturday even though there is so much work to be done. The individual being sacked argues that his outward casualness has nothing to do with his concern for the company—he works quite hard during the day. Working on Saturday is no problem, but he can see no reason for it, since his work is current. Furthermore, any overtime would add to the company's payroll but not directly help the company solve its problems. To the boss, however, this casual attitude is inconsistent with what he expects of his employees. Thus he sacks the individual.

Now, let's look at another situation. An individual is called into his boss's office and told that he is being fired. The reason? "Things simply haven't worked out as we had hoped. You might be happier elsewhere." "But what have I done wrong?" the employee asks. The answer? "Nothing we can really put our finger on. It's as much a matter of style as result. After all, some like apple pie and some don't. Sorry."

Here we have two different sackings and two totally different sources of frustration. Let's analyze them and see the effect each will have on the sacked individual. In the first example, the individual has, according to the boss, done something wrong. Right or wrong, the boss feels the individual is simply out of step with the company. And he tells him specifically what he does not like. It's a personality problem and no more. It might also have been the inability to type fast enough or a lack of technical know-how. The point is the problem is something specific, something the indivdual can understand, identify, and evaluate. The sackee now faces the prospect of having to leave the company, since he was not offered a choice.

Could the individual have turned the situation around by promising to change—to work on Saturday and make every effort to satisfy the boss's image of a "good employee"? Possibly, if the boss believed that a change in personality was possible. The individual might have promised anything to keep his job and thus give himself time to look for another position. He may have argued a specific point and perhaps convinced the boss to give him a second chance. Even if the boss refused, the sacked individual at least understands the whys and wherefores of his demise. He can deal with it in some concrete way. He may use this experience to his advantage and select an employer who will find his personality less objectionable. In short, he has a handle on the problem and can deal with it constructively.

One of the ways he'll deal with it initially is by showing some sign of aggressive behavior—a natural response when people are confronted by frustrating events. If the boss had given the individual a second chance, the individual would have felt passive frustration; that is, some blockage of his progress but, at least for the moment, no apparent danger. But blockage coupled with the threat of danger produces active frustration, and aggression is likely to reveal itself. How? Through anger, cursing, a punch in the nose, a brick through a window. Sometimes aggressive behavior is more subtle, revealing itself in ways we are not openly aware of—in the things we say and how we say them (making innuendoes), in gossip or lack of cooperation.

The emotional impact on the individual may not be destructive. The sackee may be disappointed, angry, worried about how quickly he can find another job, or concerned about the effect his sacking will have on future employment opportunities. But he may give only slight consideration to his personality traits. The individual may consider his personality perfectly acceptable and decide that what is really wrong here is not himself but the boss.

Of course, if this same situation has arisen before—if there seems to be a history of sackings because of personality problems—the individual is well advised to take a more serious look at himself and the problems resulting from his personality. He is still faced with the alternatives of doing something or doing nothing, but he may begin to suspect that doing nothing will produce the same results as in the past.

Now, let's look at our second example. Here the individual has nothing concrete to challenge and nothing specific to defend. He doesn't know whether his sacking is due to a personality problem, lack of ability, poor performance and potential, poor taste in clothes, or bad breath. In the absence of specifics, what is likely to happen? The individual begins to *suspect* the worst. He begins to imagine all sorts of bad things about himself. The individual finds it hard to discover a single positive trait, and his feelings of self-worth reach an all-time low. He may fight it at first, not wanting to admit that these suspicions are true. Yet the fact remains that he has been sacked. What follows can be disastrous.

Such an individual suddenly begins to see himself as his own worst enemy. *He* is the threat to his own future—or so it *seems*. How horrible! What can he do? What should he do? He thinks about all the people working in the company, how many of them are incompetent and uncaring. He feels certain that he isn't one of them. So how is it that they managed to keep their jobs and he couldn't? And what does he tell his spouse? That he doesn't know why he was sacked? That's not going to be very believable, is it? So he makes up some story about personality conflict or jealousy, or some other excuse that doesn't convince anyone and that casts even more doubt on the circumstances surrounding his sacking. The problem gets worse and worse, and he gets in deeper and deeper.

What does such an individual tell prospective employers? That he doesn't know why he was fired? That's hardly an *effective* job-hunting approach. What is the prospective employer going to think? That the candidate is covering up. And when the individual gets that next job he'll begin to wonder when *it* will strike again, whatever *it* is. It is difficult to feel confident, exuberant, and optimistic in the face of this cloud of uncertainty.

Much as in the other example, the individual has to consider that the sacking may not have been his fault. In other words, he should not assume the worse. If he has been doing his job well, meeting deadlines, performing satisfactorily to the best of his knowledge, and hasn't run into any significant problems, he must assume that the causes fall into that intangible area of personality, someone's subjective evaluation of his potential, some political hassle he knows nothing about, or even some reorganization of functions which simply started with him. The fact is his boss may be in hot water, pressed for results he can't deliver, and the sackee becomes a scapegoat. When an employee is not given specifics, he's been victimized for sure. But he should not let it damage his confidence.

What can be done in both these situations is this: Don't let them sack you; resign instead. There is no advantage to a company in firing anyone, and it is always better to allow an employee to resign. If your employer hasn't thought it through very well, explain that by resigning you take the pressure off. The company doesn't have to come up with reasons to fire you or worry that you are going to get unemployment benefits from day one. Your resignation all but assures that you aren't going to sue the company for impugning your character or ability. What you really want is to be able to face your next employer (or a prospective employer) without a cloud of doubt over your head. You resigned because you weren't progressing well enough, didn't like the work, encountered a policy dispute—whatever. The most common reason given is the desire for more challenging work. Such a reason implies that you are an aggressive go-getter, and this can be very appealing to prospective employers.

Job Loss and the Hierarchy of Needs

Much of the anxiety people feel when they are sacked is caused by their fear that they will be unable to satisfy needs that are important to them. A person whose social, personal, career, and financial goals are lofty will feel much greater anxiety than the underachiever or the individual who has set very few goals short of subsistence for himself.

What are the basic human needs that are jeopardized

when we are sacked? Let's categorize a few with the understanding that such needs are often fluid and overlapping and that our drives are directed toward satisfying them.

We'll begin with the basic need for *food on the table and clothes on our back.* We need to eat, protect ourselves from the cold, pay our bills, meet our daily obligations to family and friends, rest, and keep our health. And when we are sacked, the first thing we worry about is satisfying these basics. Keeping the roof over our head and food on our table and keeping the bill collector from the door are real concerns. The loss of a job immediately puts these needs into jeopardy. It forces us into a footrace with savings or investments; it hits our pocketbook and even places a strain on relations with family, close friends, and associates.

When our need for food on the table and clothes on our back is satisfied or reasonably secure, we turn to the *fair play* need. This is our need for a fair break out of life. We are highly dependent on our boss and our job and in positions of little leverage. Thus we need to know that we are being dealt with fairly and aboveboard, that the cards are not stacked against us arbitrarily, that our work is being evaluated without bias or political infighting. And we want to know that we will get the fairest possible break when our former employers give us references and speak about us.

The next need we concern ourselves with is *social acceptance*—being one of the guys. As human beings we have social needs; we want a sense of belonging, of being accepted by our friends and work associates. We strive to achieve the support of a cohesive work group. When we are excluded, shunned, made to feel like an outsider, we become antagonistic, uncooperative, even resistant to other people and other ideas.

One of the first things that happens when a person is sacked is the gradual disappearance of friendship ties with former co-workers. Once in a while some of these friendships continue, but usually they do not. Friends may shun a sacked person whose financial and professional status is in question. A number of executives with whom I have worked told me of long-standing friendships which suddenly ended because they lost their jobs. The experience caused them, their wives, and their children disappointment and heartache.

When we are reasonably certain that we have satisfied our need for social acceptance, we turn our motivational attention toward the *satisfaction of our ego*. This is the need which takes a terrific pounding after we have been sacked. Why? Because it is our need for self-esteem, for a sense of independence and confidence. This is our need to build a strong professional reputation, which includes status and recognition. Even when we are employed and operating at our fullest physical and emotional capacity, we never seem to fully satisfy this need. Being sacked makes such a need difficult if not impossible to satisfy. So be prepared for some rough times where ego needs are concerned. Your self-esteem is likely to get a real bruising.

Our final need is for *self-fulfillment*. This is our highest and loftiest need, the need to realize our destiny, the fullest range of our potential, the ultimate in independence and emotional stability, recognition and assertiveness because we are who we are. Needless to say, this is a difficult need to satisfy under the most supportive of circumstances. When we lose our job, it is almost impossible to fulfill.

Thus being sacked affects our most basic needs as individuals. When we are suddenly forced to think about how to keep the roof over our head we have little concern about our destiny in this life. When our ego has taken a pretty good trouncing, it's hard to think about social acceptance, which may only give us more worry and grief. Be prepared for these emotional upsets and understand their place in your personal hierarchy of needs.

The most comforting thought you can have when you have been sacked is that the hurts and emptiness, the uncertainties and the unfulfilled needs are natural and predictable. You aren't losing your grip (at least you aren't if you gain control over your emotions). If you're behaving in ways that are of concern to your close friends or loved ones, be alerted and don't insist that *they're* under strain. Above all, realize that your feelings are normal and can even help motivate you to resolve your problems.

Adjustive Reactions to Being Sacked

There are certain unproductive behaviors associated with frustrating stress which psychologists call adjustive reactions. That is, under certain kinds of stress such as the anxiety and frustration of job loss, we tend to put greater distance between ourselves and the source of our pain. Often, we aren't even aware of the games we play, but others may be. In any case, don't ignore the possibility that you may be engaging in self-defeating behavior.

Compensation is one of the most common adjustive reactions. In order to make up for having been sacked, the individual devotes himself with incredible energy to cleaning the house or tending the garden while waiting to hear about a job or even to avoid job hunting. The individual may devote considerable time and attention to a hobby or throw himself into work for a social or professional organization. Why? To make up for his feelings of inadequacy—to do something so well that it overshadows the pain of having been sacked.

Conversion is another common adaptive reaction. The individual translates his emotional conflicts into physical ailments—headaches, stomach problems, shortness of breath, loss of appetite, even high fever. Simply stated, emotional conflicts are expressed by physical malfunctions.

Fixation is another threat to effective recovery from being sacked. This is habitual, rigid, and persistent behavior that is unproductive: continuing along a path long after it has proved to be a dead end; continuing to strive for acceptance in an occupation for which one has only marginal talent and aptitudes; maintaining a fruitless approach to job hunting or to work itself. The fixated individual resists changes of any kind, preferring to continue his old ways even when they are no longer productive. It may be that adjustments are necessary to regain confidence, reenter the job market, and make a go of it next time. But fixated people rarely recognize the need for change.

Apathy and resignation are adjustive reactions in which the individual simply gives up. He feels he has been dealt with unfairly, and all is for naught. There is no justice where jobs and bosses are concerned. Disillusioned and alienated, denying personal involvement in the events which have affected his life, the individual withdraws, delaying an energetic effort to rebuild. Everyone feels withdrawal to some degree at first, but when it is prolonged to the point at which there is serious doubt about reentry, resignation and apathy have taken hold. Some individuals experience this reaction so strongly that they remain out of work for years. This behavior is much like flight and withdrawal, except that in the latter case individuals begin to alienate themselves from other people and withdraw into a shell of isolation.

Repressive behavior is displayed by the individual who seems to ignore completely the difficult position he faces now that he has no job. The experience of being sacked and the anxiety-ridden prospects of reentering the labor force are painful uncertainties, so the individual attempts to forget all about them. He ignores them while displaying a

carefree, frivolous attitude. This is often mistaken for irre-
sponsibility.

Another common adaptive reaction is *regression.* The
sacked individual decides that it might be best to seek a job
at a somewhat lower professional, skills, and pay level.
Taking a step backward into a less demanding job seems
more comforting and less dangerous.

Once in a while *reaction formation* takes place, in
which an individual actually agrees with his sacking and
praises the astuteness of his boss. Actually, the individual
despises those who have put him in such a terrible situation, but thoughts of hatred are unacceptable to him. So
he represses his feelings and instead expresses the opposite view.

In *projection,* the individual denies his problem and instead blames other people. He may feel that others are out
to get him because they fear his power or feel threatened
by his potential climb in the organization. Actually the individual is protecting himself from what may be the truth—
his own shortcomings. Or he may not wish to face the
realities of a poor selection of employer. Imagining that a
conspiracy is afoot buffers him from further emotional
pain. Many times this is also an indication of the individual's hidden desire to block the progress of others.

Rationalization is another common adjustive reaction.
Here people make excuses for their shortcomings or justify
setbacks. The rationalizer says, "I got blamed for the boss's
shortcomings and took the rap for him." Or "A lot of other
people will be sacked because management doesn't want
thinkers." Or "Business is bad. Many people are being laid
off."

The individual who becomes angry, irritable, or even
abusive to his loved ones is displaying *displacement behavior.* He cannot strike back at those who sacked him, so
he selects secondary targets.

Finally, we come to *fantasy,* the most exotic escape of

them all. These are the make-believes of our lives and they are valuable because we can lose ourselves for a few moments in a wonderful fantasy world in which all goes our way, in which we never lose and are always loved, appreciated, respected, and admired by everyone. This is the mode of thinking in which we picture ourselves applying for a job, being hired into a position which pays many times what we were making, and then find that the guy who sacked us is now our subordinate. How sweet is fantasy!

Conclusion

We have discussed some of the emotional trauma associated with being sacked. The purpose of the discussion is to alert you to the emotional disorientation that is natural at such a time and to familiarize you with some fundamental reactions. In this way, you may be much better prepared to adjust to the emotional upset you will feel when you are sacked. You will gain a more rational perspective about these upsets and shorten the time it takes you to move out of them. It is a matter of time, and many of these feeling states are as inevitable as sunrise and sunset. For that reason they are normal and even desirable—as precursors of self-analysis and understanding and as motivators. Facing these anxieties and frustrations, understanding them, and then wearing them down is your best assurance of survival, rebuilding, and reentry.

2

Every
Penny Counts

Evaluating Material Needs

Being sacked gives people the opportunity to critically evaluate their financial well-being. This is an opportunity that few of us take until we are forced to. We want to believe that our jobs are secure and that we will never be faced with the dreadful financial crises that being sacked causes. We want to believe that there is an angel watching over us who will never allow this to happen. But it does, and perhaps in your case it already has. It is only natural that the first thing we do is think about how long we have until our immediate cash runs out

What I mean by immediate cash is the money we can lay our hands on quickly, through a savings or checking account, nest egg, or the loose change in a sugar bowl. That is the money we look to for rent, food, and essentials such as light, heat, and gas for our cars—the primary necessities. Most of us share the same primary necessities;

but for some of us there are special kinds of things (for example, club memberships or luxury vacations) that are primary in our lives.

Now is the time to take pencil in hand and start making some hard, cold decisions, survival kinds of decisions. You have no way of knowing how long you will be out of work. It may be a few weeks or months; it may drag on and on. A lot depends on the kind of job you are seeking, the nature of the employment market, the state of the economy, the season of the year, and circumstances peculiar to your geographic area. If you happen to be sacked during an economic recession when thousands of others are being sacked as well, you might plan on a long, hard job hunt. If your professional area always has many more applicants than job opportunities, the going will be rough even under the best of economic conditions.

Take a look at the want-ad section of the newspaper and count how many job openings there are in your field compared with other fields. Look at the Sunday classified ads, which are always the biggest of the week. If they reveal only a smattering of jobs in which you are interested or for which you qualify, you will probably be in for a rather long search. Still, all it takes is one right ad to turn your life around, and that is the peg on which you must hang your hopes.

But you need to be realistic; you can't hide from what has happened. If you are married, losing your job becomes a family affair, not something to think about alone. Include your spouse and the children—yes, the children. Let them know in an unemotional way, without frightening them into hysteria and anxiety, that you are out of work and that for a time it's going to be a little rough. Let them know that some of the things they planned to buy will need to be postponed until you get back on your feet. Explain to them that many thousands of people lose their jobs every year and that it passes, as does every bad experience. Enlist their help and their understanding and you may be surprised how much comfort they can be at a time like this. Often adversity brings a family together in ways that good times and plenty of money never can.

You also have the alternative of not discussing your job loss with your children—of shielding them from the brutal realities of life. It is your decision. But keep in mind that it is a common life experience, a sobering reality. It can give your children the understanding that life is not a constant, that change is always with us, and that to survive we must be flexible, alert, sensitive, and aware.

I once counseled an unemployed manager who indicated that as a result of being sacked his marriage was on the rocks and he anticipated a divorce. On questioning him further, I found out that for more than a month he had hidden his job loss from his wife. He got up each morning as he had always done, got dressed "for work," and spent the day answering want ads and looking for work wherever he could find it. He returned every evening about the same time but never revealed his plight.

Then one day his wife ran across their savings account book and discovered that their savings had been significantly reduced. She confronted him with it and discovered the truth. Her thoughts about divorcing her husband were not tied directly to his being sacked. She was hurt because he had not confided in her, had not included her at this critical time in their lives. She was disappointed that he had not considered her worthy of sharing his problems and helping him find solutions. She felt useless, unworthy, and slighted.

Children who are old enough to understand the financial and social problems connected with being sacked may react in ways quite similar to the wife just described. And they too may feel alienated from the family circle if they are not informed. Being sacked is not sinful, and the sacked person is not a criminal, a down-and-outer, or a marginal performer. To hide the realities from children may place the father or mother who has been sacked in a less than favorable light—as though, indeed, there were something to be ashamed of. Secrecy and deceit create trauma, not the reality of being sacked. When evaluating material needs, you must consider everyone involved if you have a family. This is because your entire family's needs are affected by the temporary financial crimp in your lives.

There are many ways of evaluating financial need. One is to decide between the things you like and those you don't like. Now this may not be a highly practical way to proceed, but some people *begin* at this point. My wife and I like having the gardener come by twice a month to water, cut, and trim. We like eating out several nights a week, and we enjoy the theater and the movies. We like entertaining. We like buying clothes and we like pampering ourselves. We like to buy those little extras that make life so much fun. We simply don't like giving up anything.

Now is the time to decide what things you must give up when you have no choice. Like many people, you may take an optimistic approach, cutting back without cutting out. When you do not have a regular income, you look to your available sources of cash. And this leads again to the savings account. Your strategy must be to live as economically as possible to protect your savings account, to make it last as long as possible.

One good way to begin is to decide how long your savings are likely to last. It's simple arithmetic. If you need $1,000 each month to do all the things you've been doing, pay your creditors, and live as you've been accustomed to, and if you have $4,000 in your savings account with no other source of income, you have four months in which to pretend nothing has happened to change your lifestyle. If you can get a job in four months, you've got it made. But suppose it takes more than $1,000 a month. You still have only $4,000 in the savings account. The more it costs you to live each month, the quicker your savings will be depleted. That means you will have to get a job in three months or maybe two and a half. Of course, if you can live on less, your savings will last a bit longer and you will have more time to find work before you must take more drastic measures. Without other income, your objective is to make that money stretch as far as possible.

Listing Priorities

You must begin by making some hard, cold decisions. Make a list of the Important Bills and another list of the Unimportant Bills. The question you ask yourself is this: If I have only so much money and I can get no more, what bills must I pay when I don't have enough to pay them all? Now every bill you owe is important, of course, but if it comes down to that, you must decide how to distribute your finances. You will, on the basis of your lists, decide what expenses to cut out and what you have no choice about. For example, you must pay your rent or mortgage or you run the risk of losing your residence. You need to eat and you have to have water and lights, a telephone, and a car. These must appear on your Important list. You can't avoid that.

Your clothes need to be clean, your shirts pressed, your shoes shined, and your hair groomed, whatever style you wear. These certainly qualify for your Important list. But perhaps you can make some adjustments, some sacrifices. Perhaps you should try a hair stylist who charges a bit less. Perhaps you can eliminate expensive cuts of meat. Let the lobster go for a while; try some old standby recipes as a change of pace. These are some ways to begin shaving your food bill. We'll talk more about smart shopping later on. But recognize that your food bill is going to be one of the major drains on your fixed income at this point. You can't stop eating, but you can eat just as nutritiously for less money. This is an area you need to explore.

If you don't already have a pocket calculator, you should take some of the precious dollars you have and invest in one. Not one of those luxurious gadgets with a memory and the ability to do complex engineering calculations. Just your basic five-function calculator. Use it to calculate your current costs and to estimate savings and thus gains in time.

For example, if you have a washing machine, do your own shirts. Or use a coin-operated machine. It's much cheaper than sending them out. Dress shirts are important when you look for a job because you want to look your best. With a little practice you can do a very creditable job at home, just as you can with all of your laundry. It's part of the do-it-yourself pattern that now may have to become a part of your life. If you have to buy tools and equipment in order to do it yourself, weigh the cost of such an investment against the service charges of professionals. If you don't know how to do something, learn before you try. Otherwise you will end up depleting your precious savings if you break something and have to replace it.

Insurance policies are good candidates for your Important list. You should try hard to continue them. Keep up your life insurance, because if you allow it to lapse and it is canceled you may have to take another physical examination in order to qualify, and you may run the risk of not being accepted for a policy. Remember that the cost will increase with your age. You may also lose important side benefits built into the insurance contract. The same is true of medical insurance. Ill health has a way of striking at any time; it doesn't matter if you are unemployed. Consider, too, the possibility that being unemployed is creating physical and emotional stresses in you. You may not be at your peak of performance. Again, the risks become greater.

Take a good, hard look at your insurance program and consult with your insurance agent, who is an expert in your particular problems. There may be cash buildups you can take advantage of. In effect, you are borrowing against your insurance policy and you may have to pay it back at a later date. But right now you need the money. You may be able to cut down your overall coverage a bit, thus reducing your premiums without threatening the security you've built through insurance. Get professional advice to avoid serious mistakes. If you are involved in more exotic savings programs such as mutual funds, stock plans, and other investments, you may have to stop making payments for the time being and even cash in some of your investments in order to meet the immediate obligations you face.

Your lists should include everything you pay out money for, no matter how small. Even include the money you pay to have the newspaper delivered twice a day. You may find that buying the paper at a newsstand is cheaper, and perhaps you can live with just the morning or evening edition instead of both. Money will slip away needlessly if you overlook even one penny-saving angle.

If you are a smoker, now isn't a bad time to consider giving it up. Did you ever figure out how expensive it is? I realize that this may be a bad time to stop; your nerves are on edge and you may "need" a cigarette more frequently than you did before. But consider at least cutting down to save money and your health. It may be more economical to reduce your intake and to turn to pipes or cigars.

Your car is another consideration. Some people sell their late-model cars and purchase used cars, thus converting the newer car into some cash. This is a move that needs careful consideration. Any time you buy a used car you run the risk of getting someone else's problem—a transmission difficulty or expensive engine repair. So even though your late-model car is a source of ready cash, if it is running well and is reliable you may want to keep it to avoid expensive repair bills.

You can also use your car as collateral to borrow money. Whether or not this is a good move depends on how much the car is worth to the lender, how many years the lender is willing to extend a loan, and the monthly payments. Yes, interest rates are high—18 percent is not uncommon, and even higher rates prevail at loan companies. Banks may be a bit cheaper. But regardless of the additional costs involved, your need for immediate cash may force you into such a move. Just remember that it's temporary. You will find work and you will gradually reduce the indebtedness you are incurring during this difficult time.

There are other avenues for borrowing money at this time. You may be able to obtain a second mortgage on your house. If you decide to do so, consult with a bank or other financial institution. If you qualify, a second mortgage will certainly produce ready cash, but remember that you must begin making monthly payments on the loan.

Don't extend yourself too far. Be very cautious. Before you take the route of using a car as collateral, getting a second mortgage, or even pawning valuables, take stock of little ways you can cut back. Be mature, disciplined, and survival-oriented enough to reduce expenditures where you can. Turn out the lights when you aren't in a room; turn off the radio and TV when you aren't around to enjoy them. Take fewer trips in your car to conserve on gas. You may find that it is more economical to run one of your cars rather than two. Use the more gas-saving of the two. Develop some itineraries; plan where you are going before you start driving.

Be a conserver rather than a consumer. Most Americans eat too much, exercise too little, pamper themselves, and live for simple creature pleasures. Americans also have an alarmingly high rate of heart attack, stroke, high blood pressure, and the like because of their eating habits, lifestyle, and the highly pressurized pace of their lives. Now is the time to put the brakes on in the proper places.

As you prepare your lists of Important and Unimportant obligations, always remember that this nightmare won't last forever. Also, you may want to curtail expenditures in phases over a period of months, depending on how tough you find the job market to be. This will help prepare you and the family for tougher days ahead if necessary. It will also prepare you mentally and emotionally for changes that have to be made.

Unemployment Compensation

Consider unemployment compensation as a ready source of partial income if you've been sacked. There is a tax-supported program available in every state, and it's worth looking into immediately. Regulations and amounts of compensation vary from state to state, so you must consult with the unemployment office nearest you. State agencies are sometimes called employment development or employment security and development. They usually aren't called the unemployment office, even though that is the popular name for them. Look under the name of your state in the white pages of the telephone directory and call the information number listed there for the office nearest you. If you can't find the number in the white pages, call your local information operator. Jot down the number for future use.

You will have to go to the unemployment office and complete various forms so that the agency can determine your eligibility for unemployment compensation. Many offices provide employment leads as well; they are a no-fee, tax-supported source of employment referral.

Dealing with Creditors

At the time you are sacked you must begin thinking about your creditors and how to deal with them. Don't ignore them whatever you do. Get them to understand your problem and try to work with them as best you can. Confide in them and seek their help. You will find out very quickly that some of the "friendly" department stores and financial institutions you've been dealing with all these years have no interest in your problem and will make threats about foreclosing, repossession, and legal action against you. Others will be very helpful and cooperative. Remember the friendly ones and the uncooperative ones, and when the time comes deal with the ones who were willing to help. People who have been sacked tell me that utilities and mortgage companies are usually least willing to cooperate during these difficult times, followed by automobile dealers. But such may not be the case in your area, so try everything.

The best way to handle your creditors is to call on them personally. Look your best (not down-and-out, unshaven, and rumpled) and take your spouse with you. Explain your problem and the active steps you are taking to find work and to make good on your indebtedness. That's the key—your desire to make good on your debts. That's what creditors want to hear, and you must convince them that you are making every effort to regain your financial stability. What you want from them, of course, is the opportunity to pay less on your bill each month or to delay your payments for a while. You may even want to skip some monthly payments, but reassure them that you have every intention of paying and not leaving town. Indicate that you will pay something every month if you can, but that you need their understanding and cooperation in order to lift the threat of legal action.

Visit your bank, the department stores, the utility company, your doctor—anyone and everyone to whom you owe money—and enlist their help. If creditors are not located near you, send them a well-thought-out letter explaining your situation, the action you are taking, and your intention to make good on your debt. Then ask them for their cooperation in allowing you to be late with payments, reducing the amount you must pay each month, or delaying payments. Again, emphasize your intention to pay and your good character. Explain that you have been a good risk in the past and will be again in the future but that temporarily you are facing a financial problem brought about by having lost your job. Don't hide from creditors; that only makes your problem worse.

It may also be worth your while to visit your local credit bureau and ask to see your file. You have a legal right to see what your creditors are saying about you. Obtain a copy of the file if you can. Keep in touch with your credit standing in this way from time to time. It pays to audit your credit record to make sure you aren't being victimized by misunderstandings or human error.

A lawyer once told me that it's helpful to take out a personal ad in the classified section of the newspaper and simply announce to the public that you have every intention of paying your bills and that temporary financial constraints may delay or reduce agreed-upon repayments. If you now have loans with one or two financial institutions and if you owe department stores and service people, you might consult with a loan expert at a financial institution and determine if consolidating all your bills into one loan will save you money. Often it does, and you could come away paying one monthly payment instead of a dozen.

Your total principal and interest charges each month may be reduced. You may need to put up some collateral like furniture or a car, but it can be well worth it.

Secondary Incomes

Now is the time to look for sources of income anywhere you can. Your profession or occupation is your primary source of income; everything else is secondary. Let's examine some of the possibilities. One of the most obvious is a temporary job which brings in a little extra money—a job that pays much less than you are accustomed to and one that you would never stay with on a long-term basis. I'm talking about working in gas stations or convenience stores, sales clerking, and the like. Don't overlook temporary-help agencies as a source of jobs.

One of the major obstacles many people face in taking temporary jobs is fear of what other people will think. This is a valid consideration, not one to be taken lightly. It is not always easy to take a job at the local 24-hour convenience store when you are accustomed to being the controller of a large corporation. And telling yourself it's only temporary doesn't always help. But it's another of those alternatives you need to consider. Remember that you need to have a certain flexibility in your temporary job so that you can pursue interviews as they come up. You can't afford to have the job interfere with your search for employment. Try to get a job with the understanding that you can take time off as the needs arise.

You may even want to consider having your spouse take a job until you get back on your feet. This is one of the most emotional issues many men face when they are out of work. To the man who prides himself in earning enough to keep his wife from having to work, the thought of asking her to take a job temporarily is horrible. The man feels it is a sign of failure, ultimate failure.

But perhaps American men should begin getting away from these old-fashioned chauvinist ideas. We've protected women almost out of career existence. And for the most part they don't appreciate it. Many women would like to find some identity through a job and escape the routine household chores they've faced so long. Many are simply bored! Your wife may discover an entirely new dimension in her life by working; perhaps she has wanted to all along. She may blossom as never before with the satisfaction of having made another contribution to her family, to you, and to herself! Many wives who help out during times like these enjoy working so much they continue on, building careers for themselves. The family gains from the financial help, you gain by rediscovering the talent, ability, resourcefulness, and value of your wife, and she gains by building a new future and enhancing her identity as a human being.

We're talking here about overturning traditional stereotypes about women which can cause conflict and unhappiness. Our society has taught us that women are dependent creatures, unable to fare for themselves, that their "natural" place is in the home, out of the workforce. It isn't natural. There is nothing natural about denying women the right to personal and career development and expansion of skills. There is nothing natural about perpetuating a system which blocks the progress of women into management and into the forefront of traditionally male-dominated occupations. There is nothing natural about denying a woman the opportunity to discover productive avenues by which to satisfy her needs—which, as a matter of fact, are exactly like those of men. If you think of your wife as "the little woman," as a needy, dependent, child-like creature, you will have difficulty accepting her as a working partner in your marriage. If, on the other hand, you view your wife as an equal partner in your relationship, as one who has as much at stake in the relationship as you do and who is as eager and willing, and—

yes—as capable as you of bringing funds into the house, you are going to have a much easier time accepting your wife's secondary income during this difficult time in your life. It's all a matter of how you view your wife, your marriage, and your role as "breadwinner."

Some men react to their wives working by showing fits of temper, objecting to "pot luck" suppers and to a wife who comes home tired from work, unable to perform her "wifely duties" as she did in the past. When a woman works, the burden of household chores must be shared by *all* members of the family. For some men, such chores become a reminder of their inability to be a proper provider. They have difficulty seeing themselves and their wives in a different role—not a lesser role for him or a stronger role for her, just different roles.

At this time in your life, surviving emotionally and physically may boil down to your ability (and willingness) to reevaluate your attitudes, test them for the good they'll do you as a person, and adapt to change in a productive way. A working wife brings change in roles, in daily routines, even in conversation around the dinner table. It certainly creates different role images where children are concerned. There was a time when a father wanted his children to believe he could lick anyone on the block. My children know I can't do that. But what is important to me is that they know *why*.

Being a Smart Food Shopper

When it comes to saving every penny and making every penny count, you must give special attention to your weekly trips to the supermarket. Being a smart food shopper can save you a lot of money. So here are a few tips to help you save money at a time in your life when truly every penny counts.

The first thing you must do is forget your loyalty to the supermarket you've been shopping at for some time. Start being a bargain hound. Remember that food does not have to be expensive to be nutritious. Check your newspaper for grocery ads and patronize the store that gives you value *and* quality. It may not be the store you've been patronizing all these years. Be a comparison shopper. Try one store this week, then another. Follow newspaper ads and soon you'll discover the store that is right for you.

You don't have to be a seasoned shopper to know that the shape and size of packages can be very misleading. Some bottles have broad shoulders and false bottoms with thick glass. Some boxes are only three-fourths full. (True, some products tend to settle to the bottom during shipping, but others are simply not filled to the top.) Often the color of a container can make it appear much larger than it is. So always check the weight shown on the container or the volume if it's a liquid.

Let's look at a couple of examples of how the size of packages can be misleading. Suppose there are three packages of a product. One is marked Regular size, another Giant size, and the third Gigantic Economy Family size. The Regular size sells for 79¢ and contains 8 ounces of the product. The Giant size sells for $1.08 and contains 12 ounces, and the Gigantic size costs $1.76 and contains 16 ounces. Which one will give you the greatest economy? Keep in mind that it's not economical to buy a large size that you won't use up or that becomes stale after a few weeks.

Here is where that pocket calculator comes in handy. If you buy the 12-ounce Giant size for $1.08, each ounce costs you 9¢, compared with 10¢ an ounce for the Regular size. The Giant size gives you 50 percent more product for a 37 percent increase in cost. If you purchase the 16-ounce Gigantic Economy Family size for $1.76, it will cost you 11¢ an ounce. Compared with the Giant size, you get only 33 percent more product for a 63 percent increase in cost. So overall your best buy is the Giant size.

Here's another example. A 10-ounce jar of a product costs 89¢. The cost to you per ounce is 8.9¢. Suppose the same product (or a competing brand) comes in a larger, 12-ounce size that sells for $1.39, or 11.5¢ per ounce. The two extra ounces cost 25¢ each—a 56 percent increase in cost for 16.5 percent more product. The 12-ounce size will cost you 11.5¢ per ounce, while the 10-ounce size costs only about 9¢ an ounce. The smaller size is the better buy.

Now let's turn the tables a bit. A product sells at 49¢ for 6 ounces. Another brand sells at 59¢ for 9 ounces. For a 20 percent increase in cost you get 50 percent more product if you buy the 9-ounce size. Now let's compare the 6-ounce, 49¢ size with a 9-ounce size that sells for 69¢. These two products are going to require close figuring. The 6-ounce size will cost you 8¢ per ounce, while the 9-ounce size will cost about 7.5¢ an ounce. For a 41 percent increase in cost you get 50 percent more product. The question is whether it really pays to buy the 9-ounce size to save half a cent an ounce when the product may spoil if it is not used. Also, consider that there is a 20¢ difference in price. If you give away that much on half of the items you buy in a single week's shopping trip, you may tie up several dollars unnecessarily.

As a smart shopper, you always want to get your money's worth. When comparing two competing products, always check the ingredients on the label, noting especially in what order they are listed. Remember that what is listed first under ingredients represents the highest percentage of substance in the product; what is listed second has the second highest percentage; and so forth. Suppose you want to buy a meat sauce. For the sake of argument, let's say the label reads, "Ingredients: Water, spices, soybeans, soybean extract, kidney beans, meat by-products, pork, beef, and preservatives." Now check the ingredients of a competitor's brand. Again for the sake of argument, let's say the label reads, "Ingredients: Tomatoes, tomato paste, water, beef, pork, soybeans, spices, and preservatives." Now suppose the first product is cheaper than the second. Can you understand why?

If you have children, you may have to become something of a breakfast cereal expert. As you walk down the aisle containing dozens of brands of breakfast cereal, you may make your decision on the basis of what Junior has seen on television commercials. But that is not wise shopping. There is probably more variety among breakfast cereals than any other products. So let's take a look at Cereal A. It comes in a 20-ounce box and sells for $1.39. The cost per ounce is 7¢. Cereal B comes in a 12-ounce box and retails for 66¢. The cost is 5.5¢ an ounce. Assuming you like the taste, appearance, and texture of both cereals equally well, the better buy will be—you figure it out. You get 67 percent more in Cereal A than in Cereal B, but your cost is 110 percent higher. Your cost per ounce for Cereal A is 1.5¢ more than for Cereal B.

When you buy meat, there are a number of things you must take into consideration besides the actual out-of-pocket costs. For one thing, the meat may shrink significantly during cooking. If so, you've actually lost money. So you must consider the amount of cooked lean meat you will get for the money you spend at the meat counter. Assume for a moment that the price you pay for a chuck roast, a pork roast, and ground beef is about the same. What is your best buy? Well, the fact is that the roasts will shrink when you cook them, and about one-quarter to one-half of their weight is bone. You are also going to have fat and drippings. Thus the roasts will deliver to your table only half to perhaps three-quarters the amount of servable meat you will get with ground beef. So it will cost you more even though the prices per pound for the roasts and ground beef are the same.

Grades of meat are another consideration in economizing. All meat is inspected and bears a federal or local inspection stamp—assuming the retailer is reputable. As a result of these inspections, meat is given grades such as Prime, Choice, Standard, and Commercial. Prime is usually too expensive for the average shopper and is typically reserved for restaurants and hotels. Commercial or Standard grades are not high in quality and usually are not sold in local food stores. Choice is usually your best dollar buy for quality and price.

Now let's look at poultry. These days you can buy poultry in a variety of ready-to-cook packages, ranging from frozen and fresh to canned and even dehydrated. But always remember that you pay for convenience, just as you pay considerably more for food items at convenience stores than you do at regular food markets. The labels on poultry packages usually suggest preferred cooking methods. For example, you'll see "stewing chicken," "roaster," "fryer," or "broiler or fryer." It's usually best to buy the right chicken for the kind of cooking you want to do.

Eggs are an economical and nutritious food. They are widely used not only at breakfast but also at lunch and dinner by those who wish to economize. If you are careful you can achieve the economy you've set out for. First of all, buy eggs in cartons—they are better protected against breakage—and buy only refrigerated ones so that you do not lose freshness. Federally graded eggs are so indicated on the carton. The grade of eggs seems to be widely misunderstood. It has nothing to do with nutritional value. Lower grades of eggs have as much wholesomeness as higher grades. Grade AA (also called Fresh Fancy) and Grade A are used when the appearance of the egg after it is prepared is important, such as frying or poaching. But Grade B is perfect for cooking or scrambling.

Another way to classify eggs is by their size. Again, size has nothing to do with quality. It is not true that the larger the egg the higher the quality. High-quality eggs may be large or small. And the size has nothing to do with nutritional value. U.S. Extra Large eggs usually weigh 27 ounces per dozen; U.S. Large, 24 ounces; U.S. Medium, 21 ounces; and U.S. Small, 18 ounces. Size is important in certain recipes, particularly baking. Otherwise, it usually does not matter. One last note. Be a bit careful in buying cracked eggs to save money. These eggs might contain bacteria capable of producing food poisoning. So use them only if they are going to be thoroughly cooked.

You also need to be careful about fruits and vegetables if you are going to get your money's worth. Let's take a quick walk past the fruit and vegetable section of the supermarket and look for money wasters.

Strawberries without caps may be too ripe to buy right now.

A ripe cantaloupe has no stem.

Smooth, thin-skinned oranges have more juice than rough, thick-skinned varieties.

Greenish yellow lemons are usually tart.

Soft pears are ripe and ready.

The longer you keep asparagus, the tougher it gets.

Never buy broccoli with spreading heads or stalks that are yellowing.

Smudgy spots on brussels sprouts mean insect damage.

Watch out for worm holes under the leaves of cabbage heads.

Never buy cauliflower that is yellowing.

No matter how large the stalk of celery, avoid pithy, woody, or stringy varieties.

Avoid lettuce with loosely hanging outer leaves.

Moisture at the neck of an onion is a sign of decay. If you want a strong onion get one that is round and medium size.

Peas with bulging pods aren't necessarily good peas.

Potatoes with deep eyes are wasteful; those with green
skins, bitter. Dirty potatoes may indicate a lower grade.
Potatoes harvested in the spring and summer are usually
less mealy.
Never buy a tomato with grown cracks in it.
Don't buy highest-quality fruits and vegetables for canning
or for stews; it's too wasteful.

Be careful how you store things too. Don't put apples,
cherries, peaches, plums, or tomatoes in the refrigerator
until they are ripe. Always leave grapefruit, limes, lemons,
and oranges uncovered and in a cool place. Keep onions,
potatoes, sweet potatoes, and rutabagas out of the light.
Refrigerate corn in the husk, grapes, pineapples, and
watermelon.

Every penny counts right now, so make it a point to be
careful about your money. Many people find that even
after they get back on their feet the smart shopping tricks
they've learned provide them with a little "mad" money
for extras.

3

Last-Ditch Stands
and Legalities

Job Creativity

Most people will accept being sacked without making any
meaningful effort to turn the tide. Notice that I said *meaningful* effort. That goes beyond arguing with your boss
about what a mistake he is making. By the time a boss
sacks you he's had many discussions with his boss, probably has documented the reasons, and may even have for-
warded the matter to upper management—depending on
the size of the company, your job and years of service, and
the reasons you are being sacked.

Most bosses won't take the chance of sacking someone
on the spot because they want to make sure their boss
agrees first. Most companies require someone at a higher
level than the immediate supervisor to approve any sacking. So by the time you get the word, the matter may have
been run up and down the organization like so much dirty
linen. When action is finally taken, the upper echelons feel

fairly certain that they have just cause and that they are not leaving themselves open to a lawsuit.

In spite of all this, many people on the verge of getting sacked manage to alter the course of management's decision. Let's not kid ourselves; it's not easy. It means that management may have to partially reverse itself. It may even make it appear that some on the management team cannot make a decision and stick with it. Once a decision has been made, management is fearful of changing its mind even if the decision is a bad one. Most managers would rather make a bad decision nobody will find out about than reverse a bad decision and appear to be weak or hasty, acting without proper deliberation. So it isn't easy to reverse a decision, but it can be done. And it's worth a try, particularly when it means the difference between being sacked and saving yourself from unemployment. Let me share with you a few of the ideas some people have used in the past.

The basic strategy is to prevent the sacking from actually taking place. One of the ways is to ask management to reconsider for one of several reasons, none of which should be aimed at making management feel more inept than it already feels. It doesn't pay to point out how faulty management's decision about you really is or to demonstrate all the flaws in the case against you. Right or wrong, they've made their case and presumably they are happy with it. You need to have strong enough reasons for not being sacked to overcome their conviction that the company will be better off without you. Once people have made up their minds, you cannot make them reverse themselves, but you can request that the *conditions* of your sacking be altered.

The most common plea for humane treatment is usually based on financial plight. The argument has been made, often with success, that this multimillion-dollar company has nothing to gain by breaking the sacked individual financially. Therefore, a strong delaying tactic is to request that management allow you some time, perhaps three or four months, to find other work and to make some arrangements with your creditors. A letter to the president of the company may do more good than a request to your immediate supervisor. Presidents of companies, surprising as it may seem, often do not relish being directly or indirectly responsible for the ruin of any one individual. They can crush an entire industry that stands in their way or absorb the competition like so many chocolate chips in a cookie, but they have a hard time dismembering their own.

Some potential sackees have said, in effect, "What will it serve this million-dollar corporation to drive me and my family into bankruptcy? Can't you give me a few months to save my family in return for the time I spent here productively?" It may gain you a few months' time to look for work. Now, suppose the company has already recruited for and found your replacement. That pretty much blocks any efforts you might make to remain on your job a little longer. Still, there may be another way.

Go to the personnel office or to the individual responsible for hiring. Find out what jobs are available in the organization. There is always the possibility that you can qualify for another job within the company on a permanent or temporary basis. Now, let's look at some of the wrinkles involved in this plan. Usually a deal like this will work only if you are reasonably well qualified for the job vacancy. If the job requires knowledge of a machine or a special academic background, your chances may be slim. But if you are qualified minimally for the job, and if your prior education and job experiences as well as current company experience stand you in good stead, you just might have a chance. An awful lot will depend on why you are being sacked.

Let's analyze this point for a moment. In trying to find

another place for yourself in the organization, a lot depends on your company's value system. Different companies value different traits. For example, being late all the time could be very serious if your company values punctuality. A different company may not see it as important. The company may take the attitude that responsible people will manage to finish their work on time, pacing themselves as they need to, and that the end result is what counts.

If your job requires number aptitudes or has changed to require more and you simply don't have those skills, that's another matter. You may be excellent when it comes to interpersonal relations or verbal matters, and these become possible fallback attributes at such a time. If you are constantly having problems with the people you work with, especially your boss, if you are argumentative or have a personality that is not appreciated in this particular department, the question will be whether you can get along with the people in another department. If you are not well organized or don't do well under pressure, if you don't have the "killer instinct" necessary in some management jobs, or if you prefer to work in jobs requiring plodding rather than spectacular performance, you may find it possible to turn your particular strengths and weaknesses into a valuable commodity in another department.

The next problem you have is getting your immediate superior, the one who has recommended that you be sacked, to recommend you to another department. This is a highly complex situation. Your immediate supervisor does not want to appear confused, vacillating, or inconsistent. The supervisor is going to worry about what his boss will think of these high jinks. On the other hand, the supervisor in the department with the job vacancy may wonder why he should take a person who can't cut it in another department. And this is when you fall back on the reasons you were sacked. You may have to convince your boss about this.

Here's an example: "Look, I know I'm no whiz at numbers and as far as all the detail in my job, I have to agree that I'm just not turned on by it. But I've got a good personality, I know our products and services, I can get along with people, and I can be a good representative of the company. I can do the job in customer service very well. I'm punctual and hardworking and I do try hard. I think I've got the aptitudes for that department and I agree I don't have it for this department." While this situation may be too ideal to be true, it gives you an idea about how to compare your problems in one department with the strengths you might offer another. Obviously, such a strategy might require changing the field into which you may have invested many years. Still, if it becomes clear that this field is not right for you, a change is very much in order. It is not uncommon for people to spend many years in a field without realizing that they would be far better off in another.

Even if the reasons you are being sacked fall into the "taboo" category for your company, you might be able to make a case for yourself by convincing those concerned that you know your weaknesses and are making a determined effort to correct them. Argue that your time spent with the company coupled with this insight makes you a good investment. You might also point out that people hired from the outside are unknown quantities. They have no company experience and may even have weaknesses worse than yours. This is not the strongest of arguments, granted, but it does point up a definite fact: Recruiters tend to select against employees for promotions, opting to hire from the outside because of the weaknesses they are aware of in current employees. Outside recruits are known only by their assumed strengths, since their weaknesses are not fully understood.

Going to your immediate supervisor is one good way to begin. Another approach is to speak to the supervisor whose department has a vacancy. There is substantial gain to be made if you know the supervisor and if your relationship with him, even if casual, has been at least pleasant. Meet with him at a time when he can devote his attention to you; avoid busy hours or afterwork sessions when he wants to get away on time. Level with him about your situation. Tell him exactly why you are being sacked. Don't throw rocks at your present supervisor or air all the dirty linen; that doesn't make a good impression. Be businesslike, factual, sincere, and unemotional. Indicate a strong desire to stay with the company and work for him. Tell him why you feel you are qualified for the job and why you should be given a chance. State your strong points and speak to the question of the weak ones. Don't hide from them.

If the job pays less than the one you are currently leaving, what does it matter? It's far better than being unemployed and there are advantages if you make a success of it. If you have fringe benefits, a pension, and perquisites such as vacation and sick leave, you have an investment in the company and you could, in time, overcome the salary deficiency. Offer to attend night school and learn new skills if necessary. Willingly offer to be placed on a probationary period, say three to four months, as an indication of your confidence that you can be successful. Most of all, show the supervisor the advantages of having you as an employee over someone "off the street."

Another interesting approach is to create a job situation for yourself. In every company and every department there are necessary "odd jobs" which are never defined well enough to gain management's authorization. These are the jobs that no one has time to perform during the rush of the day. Here's a possible argument: "If I'm not right for this job and you and the other members of management have decided I should be replaced, I can't change your minds. But I just thought that we could help each other. I'm going to face financial problems if I'm sacked right now and my family will be in considerable jeopardy insofar as our house and creditors are concerned. But, at the same time, you've been wanting those old records organized and refiled for a long time. There's correspondence around that you've wanted but could never find. I also know that you need to expand the current files but have run out of storage space. You've also wanted to put together a cross-index of our customers by industry and location but just haven't had the time. Why not let me do those things? Pay me what you feel I'm worth and give me the chance to stay employed for a while longer and still do you some good while I look around for work. I won't take a lot of time off the job but I hope you'll give me time off (without pay, of course) to take an interview as it comes up."

This approach has a lot going for it. If necessary, extend the offer to other departments that also have backlogs of work. Almost every company has some "odd jobs" to be done if people only had the time. Sure, the company could hire temporaries or take in students after school, but these people don't have the knowledge about the company that you do. Don't let your ego get in the way. If you can just hang in there, you may actually work your way back into the good graces of management. You may even be considered for a permanent job in another department.

Suppose they cut your salary to the bone but give you the job? Again, take it. It's better than being without an income entirely. You may still get to keep your benefits, which can come in handy. And you'll have the time you need to organize yourself and your family, make up resumes, send them out, and wait for answers. You may not make enough to pay all your bills and you'll still need to contact creditors, but at least you'll have some income. And there's always the chance that you can prolong the job and work yourself into a long-range position.

One manager I knew creatively turned his sacking into a money-making opportunity. He knew that the company had problems getting mail to its branch offices in neighboring cities, none more than 60 miles away. These small but profitable branches needed some means of interoffice communication other than the U.S. mail or a chance trip by someone from the home office. This manager offered to use his car as a dispatch service, making mail runs to each branch at least twice daily. He asked for expenses for mileage and a small salary. He got them, and kept his benefits, vacation accrual, and sick leave.

Then he went one step further: He offered his services to other companies that either had small branch operations or suppliers and customers in the same cities. They were willing to give him some dispatch work along with the work he was already doing for his company. Within two years, he had one of the largest intercity dispatch companies in the state! During those two years, it was rough. His wife had to work and he, of course, kept looking for employment. As it turned out, his self-employment was more attractive to him than the jobs for which he applied. And although he made much less at first than he might have by accepting a job, he gambled on the future and won.

You need to look around you and be creative. Take a chance. Use what you know about your company to suggest a new idea. Don't be afraid to be turned down. What have you got to lose?

Pride is a wonderful thing. It helps us keep our mental image of ourselves intact; it helps us reinforce our value system even when it is under attack, and it gives us a sense of identity. But pride is sometimes lofty and impractical, a dream to which we cling. It is often our way of rationalizing our existence and may even be our excuse for plodding on. Pride can be destructive if it prevents people from responding to practical need in a supportive and positive way. Everyone needs to be admired and respected, and these are healthy feeling states. But do not let pride prevent you from accepting opportunities to retain employment and earn some income when you need it.

Making a Fight of It

You need not take being sacked without a fight. You don't have to roll over and play dead. Sure, management has made up its collective mind and feels it is right in sacking you. But you don't have to agree, do you? Maybe you're determined to prove people wrong. They'll never admit you are right, but you still want the satisfaction of having that last word. If you have been falsely accused or unfairly treated, you may be embittered and decide that if you are going down for the count, you're going to take somebody with you, embarrass a few people, put them on the griddle. And if your arguments are strong enough, your threats convincing enough, and your tactics clever or overpowering enough, you may even get a last-minute pardon. Who can tell? So if your choice is to fight, let's look at a few techniques.

The first thing to remember is to keep your wits about you. It simply won't do to come out swinging, to try to shout your way back into the organization. Forget it. You've got to be clever, cruel, and cunning. You've got to go for the jugular. Do not attack the moment you've been sacked. Give yourself a few hours, days if you have the time, to get your thoughts together and to gain some composure. Then meet with your "former" supervisor, the one who has sacked you. Carry a pad and pen. Tell him you are going to take notes in case legal action should be forthcoming. Notice you have not promised legal action or threatened it; you've only implied that *should* it be necessary you will want some notes to refer to.

From this point forward you are looking for weaknesses in the company's armor, trying to find a mistake or misstep, making people justify every statement and every accusation. You must play the role of prosecutor, putting others on the defensive. You must learn to use accusative, intimidating phrases. For example: "Are you trying to tell me that . . . ?" "Do you expect anyone to accept your statement that . . . ?" "Would you repeat that again slowly for the record?" "Is it your intent to stand on that last statement as a record of fact?" These remarks put the pressure on, create feelings of anxiety, and cause others to make mistakes in their defense of themselves. If they are unruffled and say something like, "I don't care whether you accept what I've said or not," simply keep taking notes and respond, "Fine. I just want all this for the record."

Always begin your discussion with the question "Please tell me (again) exactly why I'm being sacked from this organization?" If you get a general answer, do not accept it. Insist on specifics. A generalized statement might be "Your progress hasn't been all that we expected." Ask, "What exactly did you expect?" Force people to commit to a standard, to some measurement of what they mean by progress. Ask and re-ask, but don't accept a generality. "When, specifically when, was I told and given in writing a detailed and definitive explanation of what was expected in terms of progress?" You may receive an answer which goes something like this: "We've indicated what objectives you were to achieve." If so, counter with a challenge: "An objective or goal is *what* you expect me to accomplish. Progress, in my frame of reference, is *how* and *when*. What specific guidelines have you given me which define the how and the when you have called 'progress'?"

You must debate every word, every inference. Continue your attack with more for-the-record questions. For example: "I suppose you and the personnel department. can supply the names of those who've been sacked for the same reasons I have been? Do you expect me to believe that this decision has never been made before for similar causes?" Notice that you put a slight twist to the accusation, running against the grain, catching people off guard and forcing them to give you information which can work against them. You want to determine, if possible, whether you are being discriminated against, whether arbitrary action is being taken, whether this is truly the company's policy and practice, and exactly what precedent there is for such action. The question which must be posed over and over is "Exactly what have I done?" Try to get the supervisor to be quantitative about it; force him to be precise. When he cannot be, you gain the advantage. You can then take your case to upper management that the company is being arbitrary and unfair by sacking someone for "flagrant generalities."

Another approach is to argue that you were not given sufficient warning (if in fact you were not) of the impending sacking; that you were never clearly told that unless something were corrected by a particular time you would be sacked. Then launch into your arguments: "Are you trying to tell me that you believe *that* was warning enough?" "Do you expect anyone to consider what was said a valid warning of the consequences and the expectations?"

Be very careful here. If *in fact* you were not given adequate warning, if *in fact* you were not aware of the seriousness of the situation and the consequences, your case is getting stronger. Stronger for what? To take the matter right smack to the top, to the chief executive officer or whoever has to give final approval to your sacking. Your case? Well, it isn't based on you at all at this point. It is based on errors your supervisor has made in dealing with you, in not giving you the clear understanding you needed in order to save your job. Your case is based on an appeal to the company's sense of fair play, justice, and honor. You are attempting to cast doubt on management's methods and ethics. And if *in fact* there were mistakes by management and errors in judgment, you could have a case.

You can sense whether your arguments are making sense by observing the mannerisms of the top executive to whom you eventually take your case. If he fidgets in his chair, seems nervous, has little to say in defense of management, and indicates a willingness to look into it further, you've gotten your foot in the door. At this point, timing is critical. Don't overplay your hand. Let me repeat that for emphasis: *Don't overplay your hand.* You are at a very delicate stage of negotiations. You are asking management not only to change its decision about sacking you after a review of the facts but to reconsider on the basis of its own ineptitude.

Quietly, deliberately, confidently, and with complete control over your emotions, state your case in a business-like way. No ranting or raving, or name calling or belittling. Point out subtly that you feel you may have grounds for legal action. For example: "My reputation as a responsible and trustworthy person has been seriously impugned by the irresponsible actions of management." For irresponsible you might substitute inept, misguided, capricious, or improper. Then add, rather cunningly, "I feel I have suffered damages." These words—said quietly and determinedly—will indeed have impact if you are right in your accusations.

Now, allow me to let you in on a little secret: Middle- and upper-level managers are always worried about lawsuits, but chief executive officers usually don't care about them. They have seen scores of lawsuits come and go—most without court action. Lawsuits are a nuisance, cost money, and drag on endlessly, but few really go anywhere. In a case such as the example above, the chief executive officer is, frankly, more concerned that his management team has acted wrongly than with your threat about a lawsuit. He reasons that you probably don't have enough money to see a case through to court and run the risk of losing and being countersued. He also calculates that (1) since management at best is an imperfect art (and certainly not precise enough to qualify as a science), (2) since you are not under a contract or collective bargaining agreement, and (3) since it is perfectly legal to sack any individual for any reason that is not patently discriminatory, you haven't got much of a case. He doesn't want morale hurt because his boys are a bunch of stinkers, and he certainly isn't going to risk the good feelings of employees about management to make a point about you. He'd rather reinstate you, have a list of specific objectives and target dates drawn up, and give in to your request than run the risk of creating gossip and morale problems.

There are, of course, those chief executive officers who would rather take the side of management, right or wrong, enforce its authority, and set an example for others. These are the executives who worry about your going to the employees and having a big laugh on management at management's expense. So assure management during your fight for reinstatement that you have every intention of keeping the matter confidential and that *you* would consider it a breach of trust to discuss the matter with anyone.

It's difficult but not impossible to reverse management's decision if you can prove to management's satisfaction that (1) you're irrational enough, angry enough, or vindictive enough to bring a lawsuit against them and with it bad publicity, or (2) you are right in your arguments and therefore entitled to a second chance. But what if, in fact, you goofed and deserved to be sacked? That's a little different. If you were warned not to be late and you continued to be tardy; if you constantly missed deadlines after being warned; if you constantly argued with others and exhibited poor interpersonal relations even after being counseled—you'll have an extremely difficult time reversing the decision. Your only hope is to prove that others who committed the same errors were, in fact, not sacked. They may have been demoted, denied a pay increase, or had some of their privileges restricted. Information like this is hard to come by because it is usually locked up in personnel records.

Your next alternative is to recite your observations. Now, this is a very sticky matter, because it means blowing the whistle on the people you work with. For example, you might have to say, "Harvey and Jim haven't come to work at 8 o'clock in all the years they've been here and they brag about it. Nellie is always late coming to her desk from breaks. I can't remember a day when Harry and Steve—and, I might add, the management of this company—have gotten back to work after exactly one hour for lunch. As for deadlines, you give others extensions. Why aren't I eligible for the same considerations?"

Naturally, the strength of your argument depends on the number of warnings you've received and whether they've ever been put into writing. Even if they have been, you need to make certain that there are clear statements indicating that specific consequences will follow your inability to abide by requirements. If not, and if any of these conditions prevail, you may have a case to make to management. You may have a civil suit for that matter if you can prove some sort of damages. But on that point only a lawyer can advise you.

Let's assume you win your case with management, and the supervisor who originally tried to sack you now has to accept you back into the fold. You may be facing the test of your life. After all, you've served up a mighty big platter of crow for him to eat. And if he hasn't been discreet about it, he's going to end up with considerable amount of it on his face. Down deep he'll probably hate you for showing his faults to management and for causing management embarrassment because of his failure to act properly. Management isn't going to accept this setback lightly. After all, you've managed to beat city hall, as they say. You will have made a few enemies even if you win your point. You're going to have to toe the mark and no matter what the obstacles meet the requirements established for you.

So you've got your work cut out for you. With time and more good work than you'd have to produce under normal circumstances, you may survive, but chances are you will have to keep a low profile and not expect much recognition until the wounds have healed. And this could be a very long time. You are faced with a couple of alternatives. You can tough it out and try to make a go of it. Or you can begin sending out resumes in the hope of finding a more favorable situation and see what develops.

You may run into a situation in which you are actually accused of failing to meet your employer's demands. In this case you are confronted with what presumably are the *facts*. Always remember that there are two kinds of accusations. One kind is specific in nature: "You're late for work." "You miss deadlines." Another kind of accusation is the glittering generality: "You don't seem to be getting on well here." "You are not getting along well enough with others to be effective in your job." "You don't seem to have the proper aptitude for this job." (This last accusation could become more detailed and then be classified as specific.)

As a rule of thumb, and given the kinds of circumstances we discussed earlier, nonspecific accusations are arguable. Because they are so vague and intangible, you can make a strong case for yourself more readily than you can with specific accusations. The fewer specifics you are given, the stronger your case. But often you may find that a nonspecific accusation rapidly becomes specific upon arguing the point. The reason for this is that some managers prefer to keep the conversation about sacking on general terms to avoid discomfort in confronting an employee with the hard, cold facts. Often they try to slough off the facts with generalities in the hope that the sacked employee will go along and not demand specifics.

With nonspecific accusations, you can argue that certain matters were judgmental in nature and not a breach of conduct or irresponsible. You could even argue the matter as a point of ethics, basing your argument on a code of values to which you subscribe. This makes your sacking more difficult to argue, more complex, and harder to defend.

Letters of Reference

To many people who are sacked, a letter of reference is an important document. Rightly so. People who resign from jobs usually ask for such a letter in the hope that it will show them to be an attractive candidate on the basis of prior work performance. When a sacked employee asks the employer for a letter of reference, the employer is put in a difficult position. In effect, the employer either has to stretch the truth to say good things or discuss only the employee's good work attributes and ignore the weaknesses. Most employers are highly unlikely to put statements in letters of recommendation that could result in the individual not getting the job and thus sustaining damages—that is, loss of earnings because of negative comments made in the letter. This is why employers are usually cautious about writing letters of reference and why many simply have the personnel office give dates of employment and job title only. They don't want to run the risks of getting sued by sacked employees.

Here is one interesting approach which takes the pressure off the supervisor: Write the letter yourself, type it on company stationery, and ask the supervisor if he will be willing to sign it. If you are not flamboyant and if you emphasize areas of strength which the supervisor feels comfortable in endorsing, he may well sign the letter and be done with it. Company policy, however, may dictate that a copy be sent to personnel for your permanent file. Some companies allow only their legal counsel or the personnel officer to write such letters. In such cases, you need to convince your supervisor to go to bat for you and recommend that a letter be written which does not weaken the company's position or open it to lawsuits.

Remember too that someday in the future you may need to use your present employer as a reference. Some prospective employers are not content with a letter of reference. They like to make a personal telephone call to the immediate supervisor and chat with him. The prospective employer knows the supervisor will probably not say anything openly damaging. Why then does he call? He listens very carefully to the inflection, hesitation, enthusiasm (or lack of it) in the supervisor's voice and from those clues begins to read between the lines. That is one of the reasons why your last days on the job may be important to you later on. Sometimes you are given several weeks' notice of your sacking. Some employees become so embittered that they intentionally lose mail, destroy important files, misfile important documents, or make other errors that create hours of trouble for someone else. Or they may write nasty letters to vendors, order all manner of supplies, treat customers badly in the hope of hurting the company, or take records and information they feel may be useful on their next job. These are some of the reasons employers usually sack employees on the spot.

Again, these are the alternatives you face. Some sacked employees want to be remembered as hardworking, dedicated people right down to the last to prove that they have been wrongly sacked. Others want to impress their bitterness and disappointment on the people who they feel have hurt them professionally and personally. In a "lame duck" employment situation, in which you have been given notice of your sacking and perhaps 30 days to find work, it is obviously difficult to remain dedicated to the job. This is, as they say, "dead time"—leading to nothing except leaving. You can continue to work hard or you can slack off and leave as soon as possible. Again, the choice is yours once you have considered the consquences.

Discrimination

Discrimination has been a popular topic since the civil rights law was passed over a decade ago. Discrimination is, of course, associated with minority groups, but it need not necessarily be so. Employers can discriminate against anyone at any time for any reason; you need not be a minority member to be the target. Before you charge an employer with discriminatory acts, be sure you are on solid ground. Otherwise, you are going to make yourself look foolish in everyone's eyes and prove that your sacking was quite justified.

If you suspect that you are truly being discriminated against, you need to analyze your case from several points of view. First, ask yourself why the employer is discriminating against you if in fact he is for some reason. Be objective about it. If you are a member of a minority group, it may be all too easy to identify why: the employer simply doesn't like your race, creed, color, or sex. Well, that's a clear case of prejudice, of course. But sometimes minority people assume that they are being sacked because of their race or color when that is not the case. Some minority members have learned to think this way as a result of the discrimination they've faced most of their lives. But they shouldn't hide behind that. It isn't productive. Often people simply haven't done the job well or have messed up in some way that has nothing to do with race or color, religion or sex. True, it may have, but consider too that it may not.

No one likes to admit having messed up on a job; it's painful. And being able to say that you weren't given a chance because of your minority status does help you save face with family and friends. Fine, tell them what you like. But if you know the problem had nothing to do with your race or color or other minority status, figure out how to correct your faults and strive to do better next time. Make a clear, objective effort to do so; it won't happen unless you make it happen. It's your responsibility.

Another way to find out whether discriminatory practices are being directed toward you is to observe how other employees are being dealt with under similar conditions. If you are a white Anglo-Saxon male, it is difficult to level a charge of discrimination and make it stick. You may be involved in a personality conflict with your boss or someone higher, but in the strict legal sense it's not discrimination. Simply stated, if you are not treated as well as others or if you are treated differently from others and that difference threatens your job, reputation, pay, or chances for advancement, you may be staring down the smoking barrel of discrimination.

If you are the white Anglo-Saxon male we just spoke about and you approach your supervisor and ask him why he is discriminating against you, he'll probably laugh in your face. But if you are a minority person, your charge of discrimination (real or imagined) leads management to fear you will file suit with government agencies such as the Equal Employment Opportunity Commission. The employer smells trouble when that happens. The chief executive officer may not be afraid of civil suits he is fairly certain he can win, but he does not like the government snooping around in his business. So you may find that an open confrontation is your best strategy. Your indignation, your honest and sincere humiliation over such tactics, and your insistence that you be allowed to continue in employment become powerful arguments, particularly when management faces the specter of government intervention.

Along this same line of thinking, some employees threaten to go to the IRS or Department of Labor or some other regulatory agency to blow the whistle on the company for illegal or questionable practices. This is raw, naked blackmail, or course, and it's usually a losing game. No company is going to admit its wrongdoing to a sacked employee who has nothing to lose by blowing the whistle. Giving in to the employee at such a time is a blank check for the employee to run the show. Management is unlikely to give in to this kind of pressure. So regardless of the confidential letters you've secretly photocopied and the rest of the dirt you think you've collected, don't waste your time.

4

How to
Market Yourself:
The Resume

The Resume—Controversial in Form and Use

One of the most controversial tools in employment is the resume. It has become the most commonly used device of job hunters. Often, companies will accept a well-written resume instead of an employment application, at least in the early stages of screening. Its broad popularity has made it an indispensable part of job hunting.

Despite their wide use, most resumes do not differ very much in the basic facts presented. They do vary, however, in length and style of preparation. Some are typed on one sheet of paper. Indeed, many job hunters take great pride in being able to reduce their resumes to a single page. Other resumes are elaborate. They are bound, contain a photo reproduction of the job hunter, or are printed on high-quality paper instead of being photocopied.

In my 20 years in executive and management recruitment and the recruitment of clerical and professional personnel, I have never known one individual who had the necessary qualifications but was passed over because of a *faulty* resume. Still, there are some practices to be avoided.

Common Faults of Resumes

My particular view on resumes may or may not be shared by other professionals in the field. Let's begin by looking at the primary use of the resume: to tell about your personal, educational, occupational, and social background and indicate your ability to perform the job for which the company is recruiting manpower. A secondary use of the resume is to give some indication of your potential.

Do not attempt to edit your resume to one page if doing so inhibits you from describing those experiences which you feel are particularly applicable to a prospective employer. If you think of the resume as a marketing tool and if you think of yourself as the product being marketed, you will see the resume in a somewhat different light. Remember too that the resume is not a tool of the employer. It is a tool of the applicant. You are the creator and sender; the employer is the recipient and reader. But the length of the resume is a matter of convenience to the reader. Make sure that the length does not become burdensome to recruiters, who will read dozens if not hundreds of resumes during any given recruitment campaign. Facing all these resumes, the recruiter may decide to seriously consider only those which provide him with a brief summary of the key points in which he is interested. The rest will be read if there is time. If the recruiter decides to read every resume, he is likely to scan lengthy ones first, sorting them into various categories according to their content.

It seems, then, that we have discovered two guidelines in our initial consideration of the resume. First, it must tell the recruiter in what ways the job hunter can meet the employer's requirements. Second, it must do so through a presentation that is brief enough not to be scanned or given only passing attention. The resume won't do you any good if no one reads it.

Simple, you say. All you need to do is write one sentence on a piece of paper: "I can do the job." Says who? It isn't enough for you to believe you can do the job. You must convince the recruiter. And the way in which you convince the recruiter is to demonstrate your expertise on the basis of the applicable educational and professional experiences. I use the word "convince" advisedly. Recruiters are horse traders at heart. They're hard to convince because they've been fooled so many times—taken in by slickly produced resumes and fast-talking applicants who can make a peanut sound like a peanut butter sandwich. They've seen incredibly complex screening, testing, and interviewing techniques turn up losers. They've argued and debated the value of the behavioral approach to interviewing and screening while watching foremen use the "gut feel" approach ("I like the applicant; don't ask me why but I think he can do the job").

Recruiters are under pressure by line management to produce good candidates, successful employees who are dedicated, intelligent, hardworking, and willing to remain with the company for life. That's all line management wants! If a recruiter could guarantee that kind of employee, he would be famous and incredibly wealthy. You can see why recruiters are hard to convince. When an employee fails, no one questions the training methods used or the kind of environment in which the employee worked. No one wonders if the management style was defeating to the employee. The first question usually asked is "What's the matter with our recruitment people?" The question is asked even though line management has had a part in screening and interviewing the individual. When this fact is brought to their attention, line managers will argue, "We picked the best of a bad lot. What choice did we have?"

In this context, *convincing* recruiters or prospective employers is really a matter of persuading them to call you in for an interview or at least to consider you as a viable candidate for the job. Here are some guidelines on packaging your resume to get that interview.

Keep the resume simple. Recruitment executives usually shun elaborate resumes, which waste too much space with matters that smack of "show biz" and require careful analysis to block out misleading impressions and cut through to the facts at hand. Professional recruiters often are amazed at the amount of money, time, and energy expended to "doll up" a resume and hopefully dazzle the potential employer. What counts is content; nothing takes its place.

Make sure the resume is legible. If it can't be read, it won't do you any good. So another consideration is a neatly prepared, easily read document. A typed resume is preferable to one that is printed by hand. It is more legible and more in keeping with common practice. Spelling is another important item. Nothing can be misspelled if you are going to make the proper impression. It is important to show the employer that you have taken pains in preparing your resume and that it is something you are proud of. You convey that it is important by taking care to make it perfect.

Avoid poor copies. Resumes that are wrinkled or difficult to read simply make a poor impression. "To Whom It May Concern" resumes are strictly out. These are the kinds that are copied by the dozen and sent to every want ad in the Sunday newspaper. Such resumes are either too general to be of use or, if more specific, inappropriate. Sometimes these resumes have a post office box or name of a company typed in at the top. That doesn't work either. It is clear that the job hunter is involved in a mass mailing, and busy recruiters don't appreciate that. All recruiters believe that their ad is the most important one in the newspaper or trade publication, and they hope that applicants will feel the same way. They are interested in applicants who seriously have evaluated their appropriateness for the position. Mass mailings rarely work, because they aren't appreciated and more often than not they don't hit the mark.

Keep your dates straight. When you list dates of employment, make sure they don't overlap (unless you really worked for two places at once) and *account for all lapses of employment.* Don't ignore them. Explain what you did and why to fill in the gaps. Nothing disturbs a recruiter more or casts more doubt upon your legitimacy than unexplained periods of unemployment.

Take the guesswork out of the resume. Early in the resume make it clear exactly what type of work you are seeking and for which you feel qualified. Some resumes are so general and the work history so varied that it is impossible to tell what career path the individual wishes to follow. Also remember that large companies may be advertising for more than one job at a time. So be explicit about the type of work you want. Don't assume that the recruiter will be able to tell what you are looking for on the basis of your work background. After all, you might be changing fields or feel that your generalist background qualifies you for any reasonable job vacancy.

Keep irrelevant facts out of the resume. Coming to the point is a virtue in resume writing. If you are a high school or college graduate no one really cares what elementary school you attended, what boy or girl scout troop you belonged to, or even what your hobbies are. If the facts in your resume don't help you convince a recruiter that you should be considered for the job, omit them.

Stay away from sensitive subjects. If you are deeply involved with a political party, a local political issue, or an activist group, keep it out of your resume. You may offend someone who is in a position of doing you some good. Your resume may be reviewed by someone who holds exactly the opposite view. Of course, it may be unethical and even discriminatory to reject a resume on such grounds, but it's done. Recruiters can easily get away with it by arguing that they simply did not feel your resume indicated the strength and stability they wanted.

One resume received by the employment office of a steel mill in northern Indiana is a case in point. The job hunter indicated that he was active in environmental affairs, president of the local environmental protection association, and a member of several consumer organizations and political groups that were known for supporting issues unfavorable to the steel industry. Fearing that the candidate might become an agitator and try to organize employees against the company, the personnel officer neatly deposited the resume in the wastebasket.

Don't blow your horn too loudly. Do not waste precious time and space telling the recruiter how great you are and expounding on all the wonderful things you can do for the company. It is much better to let the recruiter find out what a real diamond in the rough you are after he has become convinced that you have the necessary experience and stability.

Make certain that the prospective employer knows how to get in touch with you. Be certain your name, address, and telephone number or answering service are typed plainly and accurately on the resume. Don't write jargon—terminology that may be unknown to people outside your present or former company. This includes form numbers and names, program abbreviations, departmental designations, and specialized trade or technical terms which have no meaning except to "insiders."

Salary Requirements and the Resume

Salary requirements are another area where resume writers often go astray. Here are some guidelines. A little research in your local library or with your nearest Department of Labor office can provide you with salary survey data in your particular geographic area. With little effort you can find out quickly what salaries are being paid for almost every occupation (except those where compensation is based on commission or some formula devised by a company to meet its special needs). With a bit more research in such reference guides as *Standard & Poor's* and *Dun & Bradstreet's* you can find out the economic and financial status of the companies to which you are sending resumes. Granted, many ads are "blind," carrying only a box number with the name of the company withheld. Thus you may not be able to identify the company or the industry in which it operates. Still, you have available salary information about the job for which you are applying.

If you know the name of the company and do a little research, you can easily find out its size and volume of business. You can also determine the industry. With these facts you can make some basic assumptions about what salary range the company is likely to have for any particular job. You have to make assumptions. You may speculate that a multimillion-dollar multinational corporation has many layers of clerks, accountants, managers, engineers, salespeople, and the like. You can also assume that this is an indication that their salary range within any job classification is considerably higher than that of a small corporation or moderate-size business. You can also make certain assumptions regarding the large corporation's ability to place you in one of several ranges for employees in the same general professional area as yourself. You might even assume that fringe benefits and perquisites are more sizable with the larger company and that long-range career development programs exist. These factors must be taken into consideration when you think about salary.

This is not to say that a smaller company always pays less for a given job than a larger one or that the fringe benefits are necessarily poorer. Many small and medium-size companies offer extremely generous fringe programs because of the "family" concept which they maintain. What you will learn from your research is the projected *ability* of the company to pay salaries in the upper levels of the survey data you researched. By determining the size of the company, you will also gain some concept of the various employee classifications which exist and thus the fluidity of salary ranges as employees progress through the ranks. Keep in mind, too, that employers make salary surveys available to their managers and recruiters, so that everyone is pretty much aware of the going rates.

You also will learn from your research that certain industries generally pay more for comparable jobs than others. For example, electronics, high-technology fields, research, and some manufacturing industries pay more on the average than utilities, insurance, and banking organizations. But the former groups may also be less stable, suffering repeated boom and bust periods during which employees are laid off. These are also extremely competitive industries where employees can rise quickly in salary and responsibility but where the risks of keeping one's power and authority are continuously under fire. The pressure is great, the worries considerable, and the pay high. If you enjoy these high-risk situations and are a high achiever, with lofty aspirations for rapid success without fear of the accompanying risks, these industries are good employment possibilities. We'll explore this point further a bit later on.

Often, employment advertisements ask for detailed salary history information and salary requirements. The employer knows exactly what salary range the job carries and within what limits salary will be fixed. The employer has established a certain experience requirement, say three to five years. The job, the scarcity of skills, and the salary which a person with such skills should probably be earning with three to five years of experience are taken into account by the employer.

If, for example, an individual with appropriate skills and three to five years of experience should be earning between $18,000 and $23,000 annually, this becomes a guideline in evaluating the progress, expertise, and salary range potential of job hunters. If the job hunter is currently earning well above the top of that range, the candidate is either too strong for the job or has been working in a high-risk, high-turnover industry known for its above-average pay. In either case, the job hunter may not be exactly right for the level of the job and may have to take a cut in pay to work for the company.

Recruiters will take a second look at such a situation before they encourage a job hunter. They don't want to place an individual in a less favorable salary category and thus plant the seeds of dissatisfaction too early in his career with the company. Now, if the job hunter is earning $15,000 or less annually (remember our range is somewhere between $18,000 and $23,000) and has the required three to five years of experience, the recruiter will wonder why the candidate's salary is so low. Has the individual simply not been aggressive enough or not shown strong performance? Or has the job hunter been working in traditionally low-paying industries, for very small companies, or in junior positions with large companies? Companies are unlikely to take a chance with extremes if they can help it.

If you have been without work for any length of time, you can choose one of two approaches to salary. You may be so pleased to get work and begin paying your bills that you willingly accept a salary less than the one you earned at your last job. Or you may feel that you must make up for lost time and therefore try to up your salary requirements. It's a game of cat and mouse really. The newspaper may give no indication of the salary the company is willing to pay for the right person.

Often you can't really judge accurately the level of a job because recruiters have described it in such glowing terms that a simple management trainee position sounds like a board chairmanship. My advice is to act conservatively and truthfully. Using the salary information and company data (if any) you've been able to collect, indicate a salary requirement close to the midpoint of the range for your particular job and years of experience.

Many applicants like to dodge the issue of salary requirements by stating "Salary open" on their resumes. That too is playing it safe and prevents the recruiter from tossing aside your resume because of lofty salary demands. Still, it is a good idea to abide by requests for a detailed salary history, which means indicating your starting and ending salary for each employer. This gives the prospective employer some idea about your progess, level of responsibility, and expertise, and helps him to make assumptions about your salary requirement.

Some job hunters feel it is an invasion of privacy to give such data or simply want to play a little cat and mouse game of their own. My advice, again, is to give the salary history. Often your job title gives the recruiter a clue about salary, though we all know how fictitious job titles can be. You must display a degree of openness with the prospective employer, and sooner or later you will have to reveal some of those deep, dark salary secrets.

Many job hunters wonder why employers will not hire someone who worked at a much higher level of job skills and authority and thus earned higher pay than the current job opening offers. The job hunter's lament is: "Why won't the employer let me take a step back if I want to?" Well, the reason is that the employer does not want to risk your unhappiness and frustration at working with less authority and responsibility than you once had. The situation could lead to boredom and emotional stress.

Truth in Resume Writing

Much has appeared in the press lately about the gains some job hunters have made in money and status by simply lying on their resumes and being hired under false pretenses. As noted earlier in this book, our purpose is to seek out alternatives and that is what we will do on this issue. Ultimately, you must make up your own mind; no one can do it for you. But here are a few considerations.

Many job hunters make up several resumes, each with the same information but emphasizing different aspects of experience. These job hunters have not falsified their resume but they have made a conscious effort to highlight certain parts of it for a specific job. Thus people who have had sales as well as management responsibilities and who apply for a sales position may take up more space on their resumes discussing their sales experience than their management experience. They do the reverse when applying for a management position. Even if they feel they are stronger in sales than in management, they will describe their management experience in as much detail as possible in order to make themselves seem right for the job. They are selling themselves, and by telling every detail of their management experience truthfully, they have not falsified. They may omit portions about their sales background in order to deemphasize that area and highlight the management part. Again this is not falsification but an effort to manipulate the facts to their advantage.

One area in which job applicants often hedge on the truth is in listing the reasons why they left their last job or any other job in their work history. Sometimes, of course, references will reveal totally different reasons from those given by the applicant. Is someone lying? Perhaps; perhaps not. Maybe we are getting two sides of the same story, with both parties honestly expressing what they feel to be the truth. The applicant states, "I left my former employer because of serious differences over policy matters with my boss. Since I could not agree with him as a matter of principle, I felt the best thing to do was to resign rather than throw the department into chaos." Well, it sounds very plausible and quite responsible, doesn't it?

Now we ask the boss for his side and he tells us: "He's just argumentative; always wants things his way. He can't accept supervision or criticism and he balks at everything that doesn't go his way. I judged him to be a trouble-maker, since that's all I really got out of him—trouble. If he hadn't quit when he did, I would have fired him!" We don't have the time or the ability at such a juncture to analyze the emotional and psychological bents of the individuals involved, nor do we know enough about the work environment to make any profound judgments about who is right or wrong—or to what degree each is right. Inevitably, the decision will be made by people who know little about the individuals involved and nothing about the work environment. And the decision will be based on whether the potential employer likes the applicant. Yes, selection is a subjective process that attempts to make specific judgments with insufficient facts.

Many applicants exaggerate their authority and responsibility when describing their prior employment history. Often the language they use is misleading, even though it is not intended to be so. You've seen these things before; maybe you've done them. I'll give you a prime example: "Responsible for the scheduled and planned issuance of financial bank vouchers to authorized personnel, checking same against an approved roster and notating for future verification deviations from standard corporate policy."

This person hands out paychecks, checks off people's names, and lets payroll know if there are any corrections to be made. During the interview, of course, the facts of the matter may come out, and what appeared to be a lofty although obscure position is revealed for what it is.

Dealing with Prior Job Losses

You may have some prior work experiences you would rather forget and never refer to again either during an interview or on a resume. The problem, of course, is that you must deal with them. If you were employed by a certain company for, say, two years and ended by being sacked, you may not want to refer to that. But how do you cover two years? You will have to explain the situation to prospective employers.

Suppose you were squarely to blame for your sacking and you know it and accept it. You can simply admit to it openly and without excuses. But you should indicate that you have learned better, are a "reborn" working fool, straight as an arrow, and ask for a second chance. Some employers will give you that chance; they like supporting the underdog and enjoy the satisfaction of being someone's benefactor. They really want to believe you and boast about how glad they are that honest people are left in this world. Other prospective employers may not give you the time of day because they "know" people don't change; they "know" once a loser always a loser; and they won't take chances. In this case, as it turns out, you took a chance and lost. That is the risk you face if you openly admit blame for being sacked.

An applicant once told me that he had a gap in his resume because he had come to work drunk and was fired. When asked about that gap by an interviewer he had two stories ready. One was that he attended trade school but decided not to pursue the trades and to reenter his field. The other story was the truth: he was sacked for drinking. He decided during the interview which story to use depending on the interviewer's attitudes.

Help-Wanted Ads

One of the tricks of job hunting is to read help-wanted ads correctly. They can be tricky, because we tend to read into them what we want to read—that is, the perfect job for us, one for which our interests, aptitudes, and experience are well suited. Sometimes, we do not take the time and care to analyze an ad and to ask ourselves some very key questions. Below is a checklist of questions you should answer every time you read an ad which you think may be right for you. What I suggest you do is to copy these questions on a sheet of paper, allowing enough room between questions for your answer. Then analyze each interesting ad as objectively as possible. And always remember that most interviewers and recruiters try to find ways to screen you *out* rather than to justify why you should be seriously considered for employment. It's not that they are embittered people who hate applicants; it's because it is easier and quicker and, in their judgment, the only acid test. They will usually opt for the applicant they find the most difficult to screen out. Here is the list.

1. Exactly what job title is involved in this ad?
2. In precisely what field is this job (sales, accounting, and so forth)?
3. What are the two, three, four, or more specific skills the successful candidate must possess (or things the applicant must know)?
4. Exactly how much experience is required? (Remember there is a significant difference between

"minimum five years of experience," "at least five years of experience," and "three to five years of experience."

5. Does the ad offer any indications about future growth of the successful candidate in terms of promotional opportunities? What are these indications?

6. What specific reference is made to education or training—degrees, diplomas, years of school, certificates, and so forth?

7. Is there any reference to salary? Is it a single number, a numerical range such as "20K–30K" or a general range such as "salary to upper twenties"?

8. What company is advertising? (If it is a blind ad, you cannot know this answer; go to question 9.)

9. In what industry is the company?

10. What do you know about the industry in terms of stability, salaries, and turnover?

11. After checking with the various reference guides described earlier, what can you find out about this company?

12. How are you to respond to the ad? That is, where do you send your resume? Do you need to appear in person?

13. Does the ad represent a job which you:
    a. want very much?
    b. are interested in but only in a general way?
    c. might respond to because you need a job?
    d. have no interest in?
    e. would not accept if offered to you?

Now go back over your answers to questions 1 through 7 and put a number from 1 to 10 (for poor to excellent) next to your answers to indicate how well you match the requirements or how well what you read corresponds to your needs, history, and desires. Remember that recruiters always think that it is more reliable to screen out applicants, so be *very* tough on yourself. You may not have answers to all the questions simply because the ad may not have given you the necessary clues. But do the best you can. Answer each question honestly and objectively.

Now get a copy of your resume and underline every section that coincides with or comes close to satisfying the various requirements stated in the ad. This includes statements in your resume on career objectives. The fewer the underlines, the less your chances of being called for an interview. This is a quick and dirty but effective way of evaluating your resume in relation to a job opportunity.

Many job hunters submit resumes in response to job vacancies knowing that they probably won't be called for an interview. Even so, it makes them feel that they are actively doing something about their job needs. If it makes you feel better to do that, if long-shot odds turn you on and help reduce your anxiety, send out as many resumes as you want, provided rejection letters or no answers do not depress you.

Resume Construction

Wine connoisseurs tell us that it is as acceptable now to drink a *pinot noir* with venison as it is to enjoy a red burgundy with fish. So it is with resumes. Anything goes. Basically, any format which best expresses your history is acceptable. The formats used most frequently are in outline form, with distinct parts. These resumes seem to work well, but there is no one right or wrong format. Many styles are popular and enjoy wide use today. Let's look at the common parts of the resume.

Objective

The objective should be stated at the top of the resume. It should be held to several sentences, carefully worded to express your present job objectives and long-range career plans. It should include a statement about your desire for challenge and responsibility. A typical objective statement might read as follows:

> I am seeking a position of challenge and responsibility as an accountant with special emphasis on budgeting and cost control. On the basis of solid performance in this capacity, my long-range objective is to contribute to the achievement of corporate goals within financial planning.

Notice that the objective relates the individual's career to the corporation's needs and points out that he realizes that his performance must be acceptable. This is a strong approach, since it appeals to the need of every recruiter to find an individual who is sensitive to the demands of the job and who is cognizant of the relationship between hard work and achievement. Notice too that the individual has intentionally narrowed the scope of his job hunting by defining areas of specialization within accounting. This will necessarily limit responses to the resume, eliminating recruiters who are seeking a generalist and who fear that the job hunter is too technically specialized. However, should the job require special skills and interests in the highlighted areas, this resume will likely overpower those sent in by generalists.

Personal Data

The personal data section gets more job hunters into trouble than almost any other. This is because most applicants do not realize what information is intended to go there. Keep the facts simple and to the point; just give the basics. All you need to include in this section are:

Name
Address
Telephone number and area code or answering service
Marital status (optional)
Age (optional)
General statement about health (optional)
Willingness to travel (optional)
Interest in relocation and geographic area in which you
  would be willing to work and reside

Let's talk a little about some of the optional items. We'll begin with marital status. Sometimes an individual's marital status can be important. Suppose the job requires long periods of travel. The employer would like to know that a spouse is not being neglected or that strain is not being placed on the marital relationship. This does not mean that married people do not hold jobs requiring considerable travel. It means, however, that if your resume is acted upon and you are called in for an interview, you will be asked a specific question on this point.

Some employers want to hire married people because they feel they are more stable and more in need of their salary because of financial obligations. While this is not necessarily a valid assumption, it is one that is often made. Still, more times than not it is a fact; married people with a home and children and the accompanying financial obligations tend to take more guff on the job because they simply can't pull up stakes whenever the going gets rough. Legal or not, some employers (usually smaller companies) will adjust salary according to their idea of what an applicant needs to live on. It's a preposterous assumption but it is made, and you need to be prepared for it.

Age is always a touchy matter. It is something an employer cannot ask you during an interview because of the amendments to Title VII of the Civil Rights Act of 1964. But you can offer the information if you choose to do so.

Sometimes it is a good idea; other times it makes no difference. If the position is typically held by a "mature" individual—that is, someone with a number of years of experience—your age will make a favorable impression if it matches the employer's image of the person who should be hired. Often employers try to hire someone similar to the employee who vacated the job—"similar" in age, background, and even appearance and personality. This is because the organization must now go through a change by bringing in someone new and hopes to buffer the change as much as possible.

If the position requires considerable judgment and decision making, interfaces with all levels of management, and building strong relationships with longer-service employees, the employer will usually seek someone more experienced and mature or a bit older than average. If the job is a management trainee or junior-level position, younger applicants are sought, usually because the company does not like to mix wide ranges of age within a given job category. When age differences are great, salary demands may be too difficult to mediate, and social difficulties may arise which prevent close working relationships on the job. In addition, management may find it difficult to deal with wide differences in age and experience in trainee or junior-level positions. Some managers do not like to have secretaries older than they. Jobs which have relatively little visibility and moderate to minimal advancement possibilities create problems for recruiters. Jobs such as file clerks, messengers, and microfilm clerks are potentially high in turnover, and most companies prefer sedentary types who will not create waves.

Most resumes cover the question of health by simply stating "Excellent." It's such a standard response, truthful or not, that most recruiters probably would have trouble dealing with one that read "Health: Marginal." In 20 years

I've never seen a resume that made reference to ill health. And rarely is such a reference made on employment applications. Yet company medical benefits are used all the time. Obviously, people age and do need medical attention.

People rarely tell about health problems on resumes because they fear it will frighten off the prospective employer. This is particularly true where mental illness is concerned. Employers are more frightened of a prior nervous breakdown than high blood pressure. The fact is that an individual who has had a nervous breakdown, has undergone analysis, and is or has been under medication is probably more able to control his problem than the individual with high blood pressure.

The typical "corporate syndromes" of ulcers, high blood pressure, heart attack, nervous tension, and even excessive smoking often are emotionally based problems which reveal themselves in the form of pathological disturbances. Few people realize this, however. And such problems do not have the stigma of mental or emotional illness. A history of mental illness frightens employers, who worry that the strain of a job may have an adverse effect on an individual who has a history of difficulties. The job hunter would do well to consider this and decide whether or not to mention such prior problems. If you decide to note it on your resume, be prepared to defend your ability to cope with job pressures.

Employers are often equally wary of physical and emotional handicaps. They accept certain handicaps and reject others. Yet many "handicapped" people work in corporations: some wear glasses, some wear hearing aids, some even wear dentures. Some are anxiety-ridden, nervous, paranoid. The point is we are all handicapped in some way. The question is one of degree. The president of the company has a bad back. So what? He doesn't have to lift anything heavy. The finance executive has one leg. So what? His job is not affected and neither is his general mobility.

It is against the law to discriminate against the handicapped when the handicap has no effect upon the job. But the fact that this is the law has not changed attitudes. Many employers worry that in the case of someone in a wheelchair, for example, there won't be adequate restroom facilities and that the aisle between the desks will be too narrow, requiring work in preparing the environment properly. If you are handicapped, you know the differences between incapacity and the ability to hold a job. A job applicant in a wheelchair once told me: "I'm not handicapped. I can do anything on the job that anyone not in a wheelchair can do." He was right.

There is always a great debate about whether to indicate a "handicap" on a resume. I say do it and take the surprise out of the initial interview. Others argue that indicating some handicap on the resume reduces your chances of being called for an interview. In their view, it is better to get the interview and then show the interviewer that you are in no way incapacitated for the job. Again, the decision is up to you.

Educational Background

The educational background section of the resume should be a simple listing of schools attended and degrees, certificates, diplomas, or other awards. It need not be restricted to scholastic pursuits; include commercial and professional training experiences as well. Some applicants list almost every training course they attended while in military service. That is unnecessary unless the job requires prior technical experience. Even if you did not graduate, list years of college attended and your field of concentration (not every course you took). Include such things as dean's list, your grade point average, and your position in the graduating class. Note special research papers or a master's thesis only if the work is applicable to the job.

Do not include nonscholastic activities—athletics, newspaper work, cheerleading, marching band, and the like—unless, again, there is some relationship between these activities and the job. Do not forget to indicate your major area of concentration. For example, if you have a B.A. degree in business administration, liberal arts, or the humanities, indicate the area in which you took the most courses. With a business degree you may have had a specialization in marketing or finance; in liberal arts it may have been communications; in the humanities it may have been behavioral science or international relations. Such an area of specialization may be of interest to a prospective employer if it is related to the job opening.

Professional or Work History

For your professional or work history, simply list the following for each former employer:

Dates of employment
Job title
Name of employer
Type of industry and company size
Duties performed (briefly)
Special accomplishments or contributions
Reason for leaving or desiring a change
Salary progress with the company (optional)

One important caution. Regardless of the circumstances surrounding your being sacked (or resigning if you weren't sacked), don't air your dirty linen in the resume. No one is interested in what a lunkhead your former boss was, how inept the president is, how enlightened the company's policies are, or who is having an affair. These matters are not wholly appropriate during an interview, no less on a resume. They make you look much worse than the people or practices you are deriding.

Every employer wants to believe that employees can deal with confidential matters in a constructive way. The employer hopes that if a job applicant is ever disenchanted with his company, confidential matters will not be aired to other companies or future prospective employers. As a matter of fact, the untenable circumstances you describe may exist in the company which is now considering your resume. You may come off looking immature and unable to deal with differences of opinion. Even if you are right, state your case in the privacy of someone's office and not on the resume. We'll talk about how to do that in the next chapter.

A few quick hints about content: Don't use a job title which is so technical that no one except your past employer will understand it; put your job title into familiar terminology if it is not easily understood. Stating the size of a former company gives some perspective on the job you held and the responsibilities and authority you had. When describing duties and responsibilities, don't rewrite your job description. Just highlight your history with the company. You can use capital letters to indicate duties which you feel are important, but use this technique sparingly or you'll weaken its effect. And make sure the accomplishments listed are in fact special and not just an indication of someone doing his or her job.

Keep your reason for leaving neutral and brief and don't get emotional or nasty. State salary progress either as a percentage increase or as specific dollars at the start of employment and at the time you left. If the company's product or service is obscure, briefly explain it in language that is easily understood. When listing your responsibilities, discuss tangible as well as intangible functions. Processing paper may be the least important aspect of the job; insuring that deadlines were met and that the quality of work meets high standards is much more critical.

You may also wish to give the name and telephone number of a key employment reference. This simply helps expedite matters. Never give as a reference someone who cannot comment on the quality of your work—personal references are worth much less than work references. And be sure to tell people you are going to use them as references so that they won't be caught off guard when they are called.

Resume Sample

At the end of this chapter is a resume format that is currently popular. You might want to use it as a guide in developing your own. The names and institutions are fictitious and serve only as examples.

There are, of course, a number of variations that might be used. One common variation puts professional or work experience directly under the objective. Sometimes work responsibilities are grouped together, with company names, addresses, and dates of employment listed at the bottom. This approach is less effective than separate listings, however, since it does not indicate in which company the experience was gained. Sometimes, personal data are listed last on the assumption that work experience and education are of primary importance. Hobbies, special interests, research papers, and the like are occasionally included, but usually at the very end of the resume. Some people also attach a list of references or even letters of reference to the resume.

Cover Letters

A cover letter is a brief note to the prospective employer to introduce yourself and your resume. About as many people use it as do not. It is not vitally important, but it does serve some useful purpose. For example, it tells the recruiter what position you are applying for in terms of the specific job title used in the company's help-wanted ad. It also provides information about how an interested employer can get in touch with you. The cover letter gives you an opportunity to make a subtle pitch about yourself and to offer such information as dates of availability for interviewing. But keep it brief. There's no point gilding the lily, since your resume is attached. A sample cover letter is at the end of the chapter.

There are a couple of interesting wrinkles in the letter. The applicant makes an open statement about his extensive experience in all areas mentioned in the ad in the hope that this will provide some positive influence with the recruiter. Notice that the applicant has indicated a heavy travel demand on his job, so great, in fact, that in addition to home and office numbers he lists an answering service. Now, if the reason for changing jobs is excessive travel on the present job, the applicant has already made his case seem quite valid. Notice too that the applicant doesn't talk only about himself; this shrewd operator ties himself into the job right away by discussing both and shows an awareness of this relationship. You'd be surprised how many applicants talk about themselves and all the great things they can do for the company without even knowing what the job is about or what the company needs.

The last sentence may seem benign but it's a power package. The applicant graciously offers to share additional information with the recruiter. More than that, he specifies certain kinds of information and in so doing shows the recruiter that he has firsthand experience dealing with progress reports on sales, advertising, planning schedules, and so forth. He selects items which he feels will be important to the recruiter, ones that may not be highlighted in the resume and that reinforce his earlier statement about being an experienced and qualified candidate. When he gets to the interview, he'll have the opportunity to expand on that point. The job interview is the focus of the following chapter.

Confidential Resume of P. L. Salter

OBJECTIVE
I am seeking a position of challenge and responsibility in the finance-accounting function of an organization in which I can grow professionally and in which my contributions and performance might qualify me for future growth and expanded responsibilities in the financial planning areas of the company, especially in international monetary matters.

PERSONAL DATA

Name:	P. L. Salter	Marital Status:	
Address:	90293 Anchor Lane		Married,
	Springdale, CA 95199		two children
Telephone:	(410) 555-1339 (Home)	Age:	34
	(410) 555-0900 (Office)	Health:	Excellent; no work restrictions
		Travel:	50% travel demand acceptable; willing to relocate

EDUCATION
University of California, B.A., Accounting, 1966. GPA 3.7.
University of California, M.A., Finance/Banking, 1968. GPA 3.5.
Title of Master's Thesis: "International Monetary Systems and Their Impact on High-Technology Manufacturers."
Dean's List, University of California, School of Finance, 1966.

PROFESSIONAL EXPERIENCE
April 1968 to present

Western States Bank and Trust Company
101 Financial Blvd., Golden City, California
    This is the second largest bank on the West Coast involved primarily in international banking and loan interests with assets in excess of $1.7 billion. Home office: Golden City, California.

Responsible for the identification of foreign investment opportunities. Developed systems and procedures, standards, and criteria for foreign loan applications and for the establishment of overseas financial credit and banking sources for American manufacturing interests.

Instrumental in developing a regularly scheduled computerized foreign money market quotations release issued to all clients of the bank as a guide to international money markets.

Reason for leaving: While the bank is a stable and well-managed organization, this stability necessarily limits upward mobility. I am leaving to advance my career in terms of the functional and managerial content of the job.

Salary history: I have enjoyed a 32 percent increase in salary during my period of employment with the bank. Current salary is $33,500.

September 1966 to March 1968

Allan, Simkins, Otto, and Caruso
Tower Building, Shore Plaza, San Petrie, California
  One of the major stock brokerage firms in the nation, with expertise in
  international bond markets.

Account executive; broker and financial analyst in the international monetary division of the firm.

Reason for leaving: To seek an opportunity to advance professionally within international banking circles.

Salary history: Upon employment earned $18,000 annually, progressing to $24,750 base plus commission at the time of my resignation.

References may be directed to Elias Simkins, partner and chief executive officer of the firm, at the company's office noted above.

Sample Cover Letter

Box 1109B
Chicago Examiner
Classified Advertising
808 North Shore Drive
Chicago, Illinois

Re: Your recent classified advertisement calling for a sales manager.

Attached is my confidential resume in connection with your recent advertisement in the classified section of the *Chicago Examiner.* I have extensive experience in all areas mentioned in the ad, as the enclosed resume will indicate.

I have recently acquired an answering service because of the travel demands of my job. I can, however, respond within a 24-hour period should you telephone me. My service can be reached at any hour.

Your consideration of my credentials will be most appreciated, and I look forward to the opportunity of discussing with you my background and potential in connection with the position. I hope that our mutual interests will lead to a meeting at your earliest convenience.

If I can supply you with additional information, sales progress reports, planning schedules, or ad copy, please let me know.

Best regards,

A. M. Ready

45 East Scenic Drive
Devlin, Illinois
(213) 555-8264 Home
(213) 555-0222 Office
(213) 555-1077 Answering Service

5

How to
Market Yourself:
The Interview

The Show Biz of Job Hunting

I call the interview process the show biz of job hunting because it gives job candidates the opportunity to put on the charm, exude confidence, and role-play the perfect applicant, the strong, unflagging, determined, never-say-die employee. During the interview you're front and center, the spotlight is on you, and everything you do and say is carefully noted and tucked away for future reference.

The interview is one of the few social interactions in which people voluntarily participate in a process that would be taboo in any other social setting: the open evaluation of another human being as one might appraise a piece of machinery or a racehorse or any other commodity of potential value. But instead of machine specifications and engineering test results, instead of pedigree and track record, we use resumes and letters of reference. (How many times have you read the phrase "track record" in help-wanted ads for managers?) In many respects the interview is a dehumanizing experience, and it is a challenge to the professionalism and ethics of interviewers to keep it from being humiliating.

There are good interviews and bad. The best interview is one in which the least number of questions are asked and in which the applicant has the opportunity to "ramble" in response to a few broad but significant questions. You won't always find this kind of skillful interviewing, so you'll have to be prepared to answer an amazing number of questions. Interestingly, job applicants for non-managerial positions usually have to answer more nitty-gritty questions about their last known address, the permanence of their present place of residence, transportation, and so forth, than do managerial applicants. Still, in some companies in which secretaries, receptionists, or junior interviewers screen resumes and applications, these questions may be asked to a limited extent of managerial applicants.

Playing the Game of Interviewee

If you think of the interview as a game, it will help give you the proper mental set and reduce nervous tension. And you will feel nervous tension, possibly a lot of it. Don't start taking nerve pills, stomach relaxants, or anything else that might make you look "drugged" or dull your reflexes. And don't stop by the corner bar for a quick snort; it may leave a telltale whisper on your breath.

If you need to do anything, use deep breathing while driving to your interview and just before entering the interview room. It works as well as anything else without dulling your senses. If you tend to perspire, keep a handkerchief handy and wipe your face before the interview but never during. If your hands get clammy, anticipate that and just before you shake hands with someone, wipe them off quickly on your clothes in a natural sweeping movement.

Some people show signs of nervousness by coughing or needing to swallow constantly. Eyes tend to become glassy, cheeks may flush, breathing may be rapid, and hands may shake. Nervousness can even affect the sound of your voice. Usually, these signs of nervousness begin to disappear as the interview moves along.

It pays to enter into some small talk before the interview in order to help you relax. If the interviewer does not realize the benefit to both of you from a brief warm-up, take the initiative by commenting on the attractive office. Or say something about having used the company's product or service (if such is the case). If neither of these is appropriate, comment about how delighted you are to be invited for an interview—say anything that makes sense, but talk. Get over your nervousness by facing it and not hiding or trying to say as little as possible. Get over the perspiring, choking throat, coughing, and the scratchy sound of your voice early in the interview so you are together when the questions get rolling in earnest.

Interviewees come in two basic types: passive and aggressive. Passive job hunters remain silent, waiting for questions to be asked. They answer questions but give little more. Even those who elaborate a bit on the question remain passive in waiting for the next question. Their function seems to be that of Answer Man. They can, of course, make a good impression if they give answers that the interviewer wants to hear and if they give clear, concise, and well-thought-out responses. They can express optimism, enthusiasm, courage, logical thinking, and sound judgment. However, by being totally passive, they limit the scope of the interview. That is, the range of their comments is confined to the questions the interviewer asks. At the conclusion of such interviews the job hunter will be able to ask questions only if the interviewer offers that opportunity. Many passively oriented job hunters decline the opportunity to ask questions, either because they do not know enough about the company's products, services, and policies or because they are simply too shy to do so.

Now we come to the aggressive applicant. This type can make an interview hop and can keep an interviewer on his toes. In extreme cases the aggressive applicant can run away with the interview and actually steal the show, leaving the interviewer with little to do but try to catch up. It's really a simple technique. The interviewee starts asking questions about the company, usually about how old the company is, whether it is a closely held corporation, how many people it employs, and so forth. Then he begins to relate his answers to his own background. Let me give you an example of this technique; then we'll talk about the pros and cons.

Applicant: How large a company is this?
Interviewer: About 750 employees.
Applicant: That was about the size of ABC Electrical, Inc., my first employer. I got a significant start on my career with that company. I began as inventory control clerk and was responsible for the monthly auditing of merchandise. That is where my data processing training came in handy, because I was able to develop a system of inventory printouts that saved us both time and money. Through it, we were always able to account for inventory movement. I got a promotion and within a year was made supervisor of the department. I really hated to leave that job, but you know how it is when you want to advance in your career. By the way, does this company ever send people to management development and training programs, or do you have your own in-house programs?
Interviewer: We have a small program but usually we send people to training programs and seminars.
Applicant: I like that. You'll notice on my resume that in addi-

tion to my college background I've attended a number of training programs and seminars in inventory control, distribution, warehousing, and auditing procedures. I've always felt it extremely important to keep current, and I pride myself on my expertise in the latest systems and procedures. That's what helped me get my last job, at Continental Consolidated Distributors. When I took over the department, there were very few really reliable systems. Within six months we had the finest internal auditing and centralized inventory process in the country. Here's how I did it. Basically, it was a matter of establishing priorities. . . .

I think we've heard enough to understand what an aggressive interviewee can do. The job hunter simply takes the interview away in a friendly, enthusiastic, and likable way. What he does, of course, is to move the interview in a direction favorable to himself. He asks a simple, rather benign question and cleverly weaves a personal story around it to emphasize strong elements in his background and work history. He covers a wide area in what appears to be complete detail. Such an approach tends to inhibit interviewers from requestioning the applicant; usually they accept what they have heard as the entire story. The interviewee who continues along that path can run the interview singlehandedly, leaving the interviewer with little to do but take notes, listen, and wonder how to regain the initiative.

There are obvious pros and cons to this method of interviewing. The positive points are that the applicant controls the direction of the interview, the subjects he will concentrate on, and for how long. He dominates the overall tone of the interview, forcing the results to come out pretty much as he desires and leaving the interviewer to scrape for crumbs when it comes to additional questions. The interviewer may end up with little more than inconsequential detail questions, unless at the conclusion of this one-person show he decides to requestion the applicant on specific points. This takes additional time, which the interviewer may not be able to spare.

The negative part of this method is that it can put the interviewer off. The interviewer knows he has lost control; he hasn't done his job. He's been overwhelmed, and his ego may be smarting. You may have hurt his feelings and that could be a grave tactical error, since the interviewer is in a position to nix you easily. The aggressive approach works well only if it is held under control and doesn't bury the interviewer.

Posture and Interviewing

A few brief words about posture during an interview. Avoid crossing your arms in front of your chest or sitting with your coat buttoned or with your leg crossed with ankle at knee. These are highly defensive postures and tend to inhibit the free flow of conversation. Plant your feet firmly on the floor in a resolute manner. If you want to cross your legs, do so casually at the knee. Avoid looking down at the floor. If you don't want to maintain eye contact, look at the ceiling or out the window—both more positive directions than downward glances. Try not to fidget in your chair; it makes you appear to be on a "hot seat." Rest your hands in a relaxed manner on your lap.

Avoid postures which make it appear that you are doing all the interviewing and analyzing—for example, resting the chin on the thumb and forefinger in a studious, penetrating manner. This is disconcerting to an interviewer and may cause him to bear down with more grueling questions in order to reinforce his role. Don't pull your chair close to the interviewer's desk in an aggressive manner. It is too intimidating and makes it seem you are ready to take over at the slightest provocation. Breathe as naturally as you can.

As far as smoking is concerned, simply look for an ashtray. If there is none, don't smoke. You might ask, "May I smoke?" but it's usually unwise. If there is no ashtray visible, the answer is obvious. The question may embarrass the interviewer or create needless confusion, causing the interviewer to either ask you not to smoke or scurry about looking for an ashtray.

Reading the Interviewer

You must learn to read an interviewer just like a quarterback reads the defense. Every interviewer has a style of his own and a method which has proven successful in the past and which he repeats every time.

You need to be alert at the beginning of the interview to determine some very basic points. Begin by noticing if the interviewer continually refers to your resume or application while asking you questions. If he does, he is strictly what I call a programmed interviewer. He needs to follow a preset pattern, and for this he uses your resume or application. Therefore, you can anticipate that the questions will not be very original. Nevertheless, you must answer each question to the best of your ability, because this type of interviewer tends to score, mentally at least, every answer you give. He is probably a bit rigid in his approach, attitudes, and evaluation, so play it very straight.

Interviewers of this sort are particularly fond of partial questions. They are programmed and they think you are or should be too. So they tend to ask questions like this: "You worked for the Tender Touch Finance Company from . . . ?" You are to assume the interviewer wants dates rather than the answer "From necessity." The interview becomes a sort of doublecheck on what has been written on the resume or application. There are few surprises.

These interviewers are also usually fond of note taking. This inhibits many applicants, who feel they need to talk more slowly or take pauses so that the interviewer can get it all on paper. Don't be overly concerned about the note taking or it will interfere with your thoughts.

Programmed interviews are usually not highly productive for the company. The interviewer lacks the imagination and the flexibility to probe beneath the surface or develop challenging questions which stimulate the applicant to show how well he knows his subject and can respond under pressure. The interview is as much a test of memory as it is a verification of the facts already on paper. So the emphasis will be on detailed facts, on a clear memory for the past and for what you've written on the resume, and on simple, clear responses that facilitate the note taking.

You'll have little opportunity to turn on the charm with this type of approach, and even if the opportunity presented itself, the effort would not be given much weight. The interviewer is attempting to fill a vacancy according to very specific guidelines. Someone in operating management has defined not only the work to be done but the kind of personality doing it.

Then there is the interviewer who does not even have your resume or application in front of him. He probably doesn't take notes either. This makes for an interesting beginning. What he tells you is this: I don't have your resume with me so I don't know how good you are. Nor do I care what you've said about yourself on paper. Make me believe you're good.

This type of interviewer doesn't care about your current address, how long you lived there, or if you had measles as a kid. He is a no-nonsense interviewer, even though he may seem flexible, outgoing, warm, understanding, and extremely attentive. He is absorbing and analyzing, weighing and measuring everything you say. He plays this game with the ball constantly in your court—he serves it up but you must deliver. He will rarely interrupt an answer, and he nods quite often to encourage you. But sometimes these interviewers neither nod nor smile nor speak. You wonder if they are alive! Their failure to acknowledge answers often makes applicants quite uncomfortable, leading them to think they have not fully responded to a question. They assume that had they satisfied the answer the interviewer would have nodded, smiled, or recognized it in some way. Lacking this, they answer the question, then ramble on and on, trying to get a response, exhausting and frustrating themselves until they begin to bury themselves with nitty-gritty details, loose talk, and answers that lack direction. They lose their composure and maybe the job.

All the applicant has to do is answer the question to the fullest of his ability. Then, when there is no response and the interviewer acts as though he were waiting for one, the candidate simply says, "Is there anything more you wish to know on that point?" The answer may be "Is there anything more I should know about that point?" And the next response is "No, that's my complete answer." Say it positively, authoritatively, and with conviction. Don't ever apologize for an answer; that hurts you more than you know. If the interviewer throws out a question you do not understand, ask him to either repeat it or elaborate on it. If he asks a question you do not know the answer to, say so. Don't bluff. Most people who bluff an answer have all the composure of a pickpocket who has just been caught stealing a policeman's badge.

You can begin to identify some predetermined directions the interviewer is going to take if you mentally categorize each question. And keep in mind that some interviewers like to hop around from one subject to the next with no particular train of thought. But they have a definite purpose and that is to prevent you from getting a mental set, anticipating their questions, and tracking their purpose in asking certain questions. Simply be prepared and adjust your answers accordingly.

Suppose you notice that the "bread and butter" questions always seem to relate to your prior relationships with peers or superiors. You notice too that the hypothetical problems you are asked to solve seem to be people-oriented. You realize that the interviewer has a high concern for interpersonal relations, and you must assume too that the interviewer is reflecting the interest of management in this subject. When you begin to realize that your ability to work with people is of as much concern as your technical expertise, you can adjust your answers to this line of questioning.

Suppose you are applying for an accounting position and the interviewer asks how you set up a certain system of payables. He may well have a hidden purpose, and you make great gains if you are able to uncover it and answer in an impressive way. One way to respond to the above question is to explain the flow of paper, the balancing requirements, the role of data processing, and the relationship of the system to the accounting function in general. But you could also incorporate into your technically oriented answer a heavy dose of human relations. For example, "When it became apparent to management that a new system needed to be developed, I called a meeting of the accounting department and explained that we were looking for a way to strengthen our current system. I threw the meeting open to suggestions. This was well received by the employees, who obviously felt important about being asked such a question and who responded with some very good answers. Giving them a role in making the decision seemed to me the best way of helping them accept the new system, since accepting change is always hard for people. In any case, the system which we developed required us to . . . ." Then, of course, you go into your technical explanation.

Notice how you've satisfied not only the need to supply proof of your technical expertise and knowledge of accounting but also the interviewer's apparently strong interest in the human relations aspects of your job. He may simply want to know how sensitive you are about people. Perhaps that is an indication of the problems his company has been having and why the job is now vacant.

Some interviewers like to play games with open and closed questions to throw applicants off balance and see how well they respond. A closed question is one that asks when, what, why, or how much. Typically the question forces a short answer—a yes or no, a date, or other brief response. Open questions ask how and why. They usually require elaboration, and can't be answered with a simple yes or no. Since questions and answers are so important in an interview—in fact, are what interviews are all about—let us look at types of questions and the direction of possible answers. As we analyze the various forms of questions, you can begin to see that an interviewer's bag of tricks is designed to bring out the best and the worst in you.

Types of Interview Questions

The simplest and most common form of question in the interview is the one designed to *elicit information*. For example: "What were your duties on the last job?" Another form of question gets your problem-solving mechanism working. It's the *thought provoker* and goes something like this: "Given that set of circumstances, how would you establish that department in this company with half the budget you had with your last employer?" Some questions actually *give information:* "Did you realize that we pay bonuses for that kind of performance?" Other questions are *basic assumptions* which lead you to a conclusion: "Given practically no budget to speak of, how long would it take you to get the operation functional?"

Some questions not only give information but *set conditions:* "How would you feel about a job offer that carried with it a salary of $25,000 annually?" *Leading questions* not only state a position but point out the expected direction of the answer: "Wouldn't you be willing to take the job if it were offered to you?" Watch out for *loaded questions,* which may put you on the spot or force you into a corner: "Do you mean to tell me that the only right solution to your difficulties with your former employer was to quit?" Notice that if you agree, you put yourself in opposition to the questioner; if you disagree, you admit an error.

Trick questions should never be answered: "With a simple yes or no, do you plan to remain here, resign, or take a wait-and-see attitude about things?" *Antagonistic questions* may cause an argument. So stay alert when asked something like this: "After all the time you've spent in management, don't you think you're ready to put up with inconveniences on the job?" *Forced-choice questions* lead you down the garden path: "If you were convinced that this company was simply not right for you in terms of your personal and career needs, you would turn the offer down, wouldn't you?" You have to agree to a question like that or look very irresponsible. And that enables the interviewer to follow up with a solid rejection if he wishes. You lose control of a situation very quickly when hit with forced-choice questions.

Appeal questions cater to your need to be accepted by the questioner and often appeal to your ego needs: "With your extensive background, I'm sure you realize that we need to cut the budget. Correct?" That's a tough one to get around unless you openly contradict the questioner, using your experience to prove the opposite. Another trouble spot is *precondition questions;* these force you to accept a certain condition before you answer. For example: "When you argue with your boss, is it to satisfy your ego needs (or because you lose your temper easily)?" If you answer with a simple no, you've admitted to arguing with your boss—you've agreed with the precondition of the question.

Questions that appeal to truth and reason are always prefaced by some phrase like "The facts are clear that . . ." or "Make no mistake about it . . . ." The implication is that by attempting to argue with the next phrase, you place yourself too far from the truth to be worthy of further discussion. The full question may go something like this: "Make no mistake about it, don't the facts prove that people with materialistic needs try harder than others?" *Problematic questions* place the job hunter in a rather compromising position, forcing him to ask a question (and thus showing that he does not have an answer). Such a question keeps the initiative with the interviewer. For example: "You would never imagine the most common reason job hunters give for leaving prior employment, would you?"

Always keep one thing clearly in mind: You never have to answer a question. You can, if you choose, avoid the question entirely, and if you do it skillfully enough you can prevent or at least curtail further questions on the subject. Of course, a dogged interviewer may pursue you even though you have done an above-average job of avoiding the issue. Suppose you are asked a question about how you would function under certain circumstances and you really don't have an answer. You try to think of an experience similar to the one posed in the question or hypothesize various approaches. Preface your remarks with a phrase such as "Let's approach that question from this point of view." Then begin expounding. When you finish, you might add something like "I think you can begin to see the general direction I would take in matters like the one you posed." Your goal in cases like this is to redefine the problem in your own frame of reference. You attempt to gain the initiative and respond in ways that place you in as good a light as possible. In short, you leave the questioner with the feeling that his question has been answered.

Not Answering Questions

You do not always have to answer a question, and there are some interesting ways out of every question. You must, as a rule of thumb, always leave the questioner with the feeling that you have answered the question even when you have not. You will find that interviewers rarely consider the possibility that their questions will not be answered. Thus many applicants for employment catch interviewers totally off guard and get away with their game quite successfully.

One of the best ways to avoid answering a question is to ask, "Why did you ask that?" It catches the interviewer off guard, because he is not accustomed to answering. In the process of responding, the interviewer may reveal his real reasons for asking—the deep, dark motivation for the question—and thus help guide your answer inadvertently. Often, an excellent approach is to give an incomplete or partially inaccurate answer.

Suppose an interviewer asks one of those self-analytical questions like "What area of your personality do you think could be strengthened?" or "What personal characteristics are you least satisfied with?" Naturally, you always describe some "weakness" that is aimed at making you look good. For example: "I'm not the kind of person who can simply walk away from a job in the evening. I tend to think about my work a lot; maybe that isn't the right approach, but I take my work very seriously." Another approach is a kind of diversionary tactic. For example: "I thought you would ask that so I'd like to describe some points in my background that might be of help to you in evaluating the kind of person I am." Then take off in a direction that you feel will showcase you best. Sometimes applicants talk about their struggles on the athletic field against great odds or enrolling in classes in school without the proper prerequisites, emphasizing rugged determination and "stubborness" in accomplishing an objective. This gives them an opportunity to answer the question on their own terms.

During an interview, you are bound to be asked your salary requirement. This is sometimes a tough question to answer, particularly when you don't know how well you stand in the interviewer's judgment, the stiffness of the competition, and exactly what range the company has in mind. You could price yourself out of the market by stating a salary that is too low for your level of expertise or higher than what the company is willing to pay. Sometimes it isn't enough to simply indicate that your salary is open.

You can take one of several approaches. One is to affirm the confidence you have in yourself and in the company's ability to recognize performance. The word "recognize" is a good one in this case because it is open to several interpretations. It avoids the need to challenge the company to properly pay for outstanding performance; at the same time, it assumes the company will recognize (that is, notice) performance. Another approach is to delay the answer. Say something like "I know that salary is an important point, but I'd like to delay answering that for a while and concentrate on giving you some justification for why I feel my expertise and interests are in keeping with your company's needs." This gives you a chance to do a selling job and to justify the dollar figure you have promised to give. The approach is particularly good if the question of salary comes early in the interview.

The interviewer may try to elicit your views on politics or make you commit to some specific management approach. Again, the best tactic is to avoid an answer. Suppose the interviewer opens with the question: "Government constraints make it impossible to operate in a system that is truly capitalistic, don't they?" You can dodge the issue with this nonanswer: "It's certainly difficult not to feel the presence of government." To the question "How on earth do you keep people from taking advantage of a good thing?" you might reply with this nonanswer: "Yes, I certainly understand what you're saying and, indeed, there's substance there." Responding with an air of thoughtful meditation suggests that you've answered the question when in fact you have not. To the question "What do you look for in an employer?" you can answer: "I've been quite impressed by the surroundings in this office. I don't know whether it was by design, but there is a definite feeling of purpose here. Do you sense it as I do?"

Another way to deal with questions is to refocus them from abstract to practical, or vice versa. If you want to be lofty and noncommittal, the abstract is the perfect dodge. Simply preface your remarks as follows: "When it comes to management style, speaking in the abstract, I tend to . . . ." Notice that you have deviously defined the level at which you will answer the question. You set the boundaries. If you don't feel comfortable theorizing on a given point, change gears and get practical. Simply preface your remarks with the statement "As a practical matter, let me say . . . ." Sometimes people preface their remarks with the term "functionally." It's a good dodge because no two people define "functionally" the same way. Some think of it as operationally oriented; others think of it abstractly, in broadest form.

Another interesting approach is to overwhelm an interviewer with detail, detail, and more detail. The strategy here is to wear down the interviewer, causing him to compromise his questions, giving him to understand that if he asks a question he's going to get an answer he'll never forget. Therefore, if he is asking a question for the sake of asking it, he'd better be prepared for a long, dry session.

Interviewers can spend only so much time with you. They can't devote an entire day to your interview. If you eat up the clock by elaborating on questions with which you feel comfortable and knowledgeable, you can avoid being confronted with questions you can't handle well. And more times than not it will leave a good impression on the interviewer. He may come away saying, "That's a long-winded so-and-so, but he knows his subject." By the way, it's far better to say too much than too little. Don't economize on words or worry about how much time you are taking. That's the interviewer's problem. Tell him what you know. The interviewer will assume you don't know or can't articulate if you hold back, so it really doesn't play to your favor.

Knowing the Answers to Key Questions

Certain questions are sure to be asked during an interview. Anticipating these questions can give you an important advantage. Remember that every interviewer has his favorite "gotcha" questions, designed to cause you to pause, stammer, think on your feet, react under pressure, or lose composure. Some are so key, in fact, that pausing and stammering before answering them could seriously weaken the impressions you make on the interviewer. Let's look at a few.

How did you happen to leave your last employer (or, why do you want to leave your current employer)?
Keep your answers professional and ethical and avoid airing dirty linen. Emphasize the strong points about you

that caused you to want to leave or quit if such was the case. Whatever you say, make certain it is plausible, rational, and couched in understanding, sympathetic terms. Some people include a statement like this in their explanations: "I thought there might be a possibility of being sacked, but people must be true to their principles and ethics. I had hoped to avoid it and I'm sorry it ended as it did." There is the ever so subtle hint that you were in disagreement with the ethics of your former employer, but you never say it openly.

You must make yourself out as the martyr without being obvious or making it appear that you are playing to the interviewer's emotions. Don't avoid the question, because if you do you'll make circumstances appear to be much worse than they were. Answer the question without destroying your chances for serious consideration. Some applicants attribute their sacking to a misunderstanding, lack of communication, principles, personality conflicts, and even politics.

What can you do for our company?
A question like this is a trap, so whatever you do don't fall prey to it. Think of a physician who sees a patient in the office and is asked, "Can you make me well?" What does the physician do? He refuses to make a statement until he has examined the patient and found out the nature of the ailment. The patient may ask the physician many questions about the physician's skill and knowledge, and the physician may feel free to answer these questions. But a reputable physician will not make claims about cures until he is certain of his ground.

You are in almost the same situation. Proclaim loudly your skills and knowledge, attributes and strengths. But when asked what you will do for the company, be careful. Few people will have confidence in anyone who makes wild claims without knowing the exact nature of the problem. Simply summarize your qualifications, explain your expertise in relation to the company's problems, and emphasize your determination to do a fine job and to make every effort to help. But indicate before you commit yourself that you want to know the specifics. That is the real difference between a pro and a wild-eyed job hunter desperate for work.

What can you tell me about yourself?
This question is sometimes used by interviewers to "break the ice." They usually ask it at the beginning of the interview. Sometimes it is done to throw off the applicant, who expects to be asked questions rather than have to deliver a lengthy autobiography. Many people stammer and stutter, lose confidence, and need to be bailed out by the interviewer. Don't let this happen to you. Remember, you want to start talking early in the interview to help ease the tension, but you don't want to talk nonsense. So begin by asking, "Would you like me to start with my personal or professional background?"
Some interviewers may have a preference. Others may simply reply, "It doesn't matter." In that case, establish your credentials first! Start with your educational background if that is where your strength lies. Or describe your experience if that is your strong suit. The point is to always establish your credentials, your legitimacy, as it were. Hit the interviewer hard and early with your big guns, your trump card, your strength. Establish yourself in his eyes as a valid applicant, someone who must be taken seriously.

What is your ideal job?
This is another trap question, so look out. You're bound to describe circumstances that don't exist in the company you're trying to get the job with. It never fails. You can't know what is really behind the scenes in the company, so don't try. And describing a utopian job

doesn't give you any points because no company on earth has such a position.

You have to stay away from the question. A very direct, objective statement is that in your best judgment there is no ideal job, only motivated people. There is no utopia, only achievement-oriented professionals who want to achieve for themselves and the company. To you, challenge, opportunity, and being judged on your own merit are "ideal" conditions. Another approach is to say: "I'm not looking for an *ideal* job, only an opportunity to prove myself." Or you might indicate that you want the opportunity to get a job you know you can perform well and one in which you can grow personally and professionally.

What kind of boss do you work well with?

The interviewer knows the manager you will be working with if you are hired. He knows his strengths and weaknesses and he knows whether he's a good manager. But the interviewer isn't going to tell you that. He wants to hear you describe your "ideal" boss. If you answer the question directly, again you fall into a trap. You could be describing someone who does not even remotely resemble the manager in question. In any case, how many ideal managers have you known? Bosses are rarely perfect. Certainly they are human—just like the people who work for them. So be careful.

One way to approach this question is to indicate the weaknesses in a boss you do not respect—such as favoritism, unfairness, bias, and lack of technical know-how to evaluate performance properly. If these weaknesses are all present in the manager, you don't want the job anyway. Even if several are obviously present and the interviewer knows it, chances are he won't rule you out, because no one wants to work for someone who shows such weaknesses. Keep the weaknesses you describe attitudinal in nature. In other words, describe a negative "model," someone with weaknesses about which everyone can agree.

Do not describe all the strengths you want to see in a boss. If you do, there is a good chance the manager won't match up completely. Then, having taken a position in favor of a certain type of manager, you will have boxed yourself in. For example, if you say, "I want to work for someone who will ask my opinion about things affecting my job," you could leave the impression that you won't be happy working for anyone who does not use this participative technique. If you get too specific (for example, "I want a boss who gives me a lot of verbal feedback"), you could talk yourself right out of a job. The manager in question may not be one who gives verbal feedback, and again the interviewer may assume that you can't or won't work well with any other kind of boss. So watch your step on this one.

Do you plan to remain on this job (or, more subtly, how do you feel this job fits in with your long-range career plans)?

This question is a bit like "What can you do for our company?" If you say, "I want to work here until I retire," you are making a positive statement regarding a work environment you know nothing about. Making such a far-reaching statement is not impressive and sounds immature. It certainly won't gain points for you with the interviewer, who knows you are attempting to "do a number on him." If you say, "I really don't know," you've failed to answer the question—not through clever evasion but through what appears to be your inability to formulate an answer.

A good approach is to give the interviewer the impression that you've answered his question by discussing your needs and desires on the job in a very positive way. What you are really doing is giving the interviewer some facts and allowing him to form his own conclusions. For example, you might say, "I would very much like to build a strong reputation in one company. I don't enjoy job hopping. I'm the type of person who wants to become well established and identify with my employer. I want stability in my life and I want to know that, over the years, I am building toward my career objectives in a responsible way. These are the personal and career needs I want to fill and this is the way I would look at a job which I am offered and agree to take." This approach will put you in a good light and not make you appear to be grasping for any job opportunity without careful consideration.

If you are hired, what's the first thing (or things) you would do on the job?

This is one of those questions that separates the men from the boys. If you are highly aggressive and achievement-oriented, filled with confidence and vigor, and ready to turn the company on its ear to prove yourself, there is a good chance you're going to blow this one. No matter how badly the particular department, job, or company needs you, no matter how much trouble people are in, they don't want someone coming in and changing everything overnight. Remember, people resist change. It robs them of the feeling that they have some control over future events. Some people gain a sense of security through working in an environment in which they feel they can predict routine events. Employees dislike newcomers telling them what is wrong. The company may be in trouble, but the newcomer, they feel, hasn't paid dues enough to tell them so. So be very careful about these very sensitive points.

Obviously, the company may be hiring you to make changes, to improve a bad situation. Or it may be hiring you in the hope that you will do the job as well as (or perhaps, exactly like) the previous occupant. Now, which is it? A good approach at this point is to ask how the job happened to be vacant. If you are told that the person who previously held the job retired or was promoted, there is a good chance the company wants the job conducted as it once was without dramatic changes. If the person "left the company," you don't know whether he resigned or was sacked. Therefore, you don't know whether the job was performed poorly, marginally well, or satisfactorily. You then might ask how long the previous employee was on the job. A short time may indicate that the job does need dramatic improvement; a long time may mean the same, or it may not.

A good, safe approach is to indicate that you want to learn as much about the job as possible and about further functions which the job directly and indirectly touches. You want to gain a clear picture of how the job was conducted before and, through consultation and discussions with management, learn what changes if any are to be made, in what direction, and in what time frame. Your approach is one of well-timed analysis and progressive, controlled change. It indicates a strong preference for team building and participative management and is more likely to gain acceptance by the interviewer than almost any other approach.

Are there any questions? (Usually asked at the close of the interview.)

Most applicants will say, "No, not at this time. You've covered everything quite well." Now, there is considerable discussion about whether an applicant should prepare himself to ask a few questions at the conclusion of an interview. Frankly, I don't think it matters significantly. Having or not having questions is unlikely to make the difference in getting the job. It may make a slight difference when the competition for the job is fierce and the interviewer has decided that the field has been narrowed to you and one or two others. When it's a real horse race, the smallest detail can be important. That still does not mean you won't get the job because you didn't ask questions.

If the interview has been long, detailed, and demanding, don't bother with a question unless it is very significant. If the interview has been marginal, a very smart question at the end might help you. But meaningless questions asked for their own sake could hurt you. Sometimes an interviewer leaves you very few questions to ask, particularly if in his opening remarks he tells you about the company's history; its general financial situation; its technology, goods, and services; the number of employees; plant locations; and general organization structure. Remember too that the question you ask will be the very last thing you discuss with the interviewer. What you say may have a disproportionate influence simply because it is "the last word"—a final impression that you leave with the interviewer.

If you feel it is necessary to ask a question, make sure that it shows you in a strong light. Raise a question that reveals the depth of your knowledge and experience. Ask a technical question that shows you are well versed, in spite of the fact that you have no experience with the company. Or raise a subtle point that a beginner would never dream of asking. It may have to do with some legal question or some acceptable system; it may deal with protocol or procedures.

The point is to raise a question on a specific point about the job. If the interviewer is an initial screener—that is, someone in the employment or recruitment office—he or she is unlikely to know the answer. That is fine because you are expected to be the expert in a specific area, not the interviewer. He may say, "That's a technical point I'm not aware of; save it until you speak with the department manager." That answer is a gold mine! It indicates that you've made it through the first screening. When you speak with the department head or the person you would report to if hired, fire off as many technical questions as you like. But be sensitive to his fatigue factor, watching for little signs such as easing away from the desk as though to get up. Don't bother with superficial questions that won't showcase your depth and that only take up time.

Higher-Level Interviews

During the course of interviewing you may meet many managers, particularly if you are applying for a management position. You will find, of course, that some managers who are part of your interview agenda have no technical knowledge about your field. Their only purpose is to get a general feeling about you as an individual, as a team player, as a potential political ally, as someone they wouldn't mind having lunch with, or as someone who would be an asset to the management team. Other managers may be in charge of departments that work closely with the function for which you are applying. They too may lack your technical expertise, but they will want to gain some idea about what kind of person you would be to work with.

You may even be interviewed by a top executive of the company who is unlikely to have technical expertise in your area but who knows what he needs to have from your area in the way of data, production, teamwork, and so on. The questions he asks will give you some idea about his concerns and the needs he wants filled. Listen to these questions and remember key points. As the interview progresses, you will get an idea of the direction in which he is going. At that point, when you think you have sensed his chief concern, capitalize on it. Use any question or comment to expand on the direction you think he's going. It's a bit of a gamble, because if you're wrong, you've gone off on a tangent. Even so, it may not hurt your chances and it does give you an opportunity to voice your opinions and knowledge. With careful analysis throughout the interview you are bound to pick up the thread of his thinking. When you do, give it all you've got. It's worth the risk.

One last point. Remember that interview styles differ. Some managers will "argue" with you, debate or analyze a statement you have made from either a technical or philosophical point of view. They do this not only because they enjoy it but because it helps them draw you out. They want to know the depth of your thinking and how confident and resolute you are. It usually does not matter if you differ with them as long as you do so with intelligence, relying on your base of knowledge and expertise. Argue with calmness and diplomacy.

There are many acceptable ways of solving a problem. Each way has its adherents and each is valid and ethical in its own right, even professionally accepted. If your approach differs with the interviewer's in some ways, adopt the attitude that you and he are professional equals, sharing points of view. You are each operating from a base of facts, experience, and expertise. Don't collapse like a house of cards, giving in to the interviewer because you fear that disagreeing will ruin your chances for the job. And don't argue simply for the sake of it, giving such rebuttals as "Well, I can't tell you why I think that, I just do." If you do, you've lost the job!

Other managers will never argue or debate a point during an interview. They will accept what you say graciously, smiling and nodding all the while, seemingly reinforcing your every word and even urging you on. Of course, if they think you're on the wrong track, every word you say buries you. Some shrewd applicants for employment will state a position and then ask the interviewer, "How do you feel about that?" Or "What are your thoughts in relation to that point?" Their goal is to gain some important feedback. If the interviewer does not appear to be in full agreement, they soften their approach slightly with the phrase "Now, there are certain instances in which. . . ." This allows them to take a somewhat different tack, carrying their next comments off as exceptional situations.

The Interviewer and You

The interview process is not a precise science. The interviewer is rarely as knowledgeable about human behavior and technical matters as he should be. The interviewer simply tries to make certain assumptions about the future success of the applicant on the basis of various cues gained during the interview. Such cues may be the individual's personal background, educational attainment, and progress on jobs.

Many interviewers base their approach on a set of assumptions about people and their motivations. These assumptions may have proved wrong year after year, applicant after applicant. But they do not bother to reevaluate their techniques or to analyze their performance and the performance of others who are involved in the interview process. They rarely objectively appraise the ability of the organization to deal effectively with new hires.

Some companies are better off hiring skilled professionals or those with moderate experience rather than trainees, because the prevailing management style and inability to develop manpower simply cannot accommodate the beginner. Certain organizations like to invest power and authority at the top. Thus executives delegate little of either. They seek workers who will grunt and groan but never reach for more. The interviewer in such a company would be wise to select against aggressive, achievement-oriented applicants with aspirations the company simply will not satisfy.

There are two basic interview techniques: the utilitarian

and the functional. The utilitarian focuses on facts—what the last address was; what your salary requirements are. It may get into the how and why, but usually on only a very superficial basis, digging for veritable facts as much as possible. The functional approach is more flexible and attempts to get below the surface—to learn motivations, concepts, perceptions, and attitudes. It is more taxing to the interviewer and the job applicant. Neither approach is appropriate if used exclusively. Each has its purpose and should be used at some point in any one interview. The interview is a social situation in which communication and the interchange of information are of primary importance.

The interview focuses on your entire life history and attempts to bring it into perspective. You are not the same person you were when you first began working; you are different because of your experience, needs, and motivations. Yet you will have to discuss the first job you ever had as though it were current and as though you were the same person, which you are not. So in describing your past, remember to describe the changes in attitude and skill, maturity, and technical know-how that have taken place in you. Deal with time not as a continuum but as a series of discrete segments. Define time in terms of your development as an individual and as a professional. Define it in terms of progressive, constant growth. This helps frame your background for the interviewer and helps you focus on your history on your terms.

The interviewer cannot "see through you," nor are most interviewers experts in behavioral science. But they are sensitive to the signals which betray the unsure, anxious applicant who lacks confidence, advertises timidity, and seems never to make a case for himself. Some interviewers are highly sensitive to such things and they make assumptions, often quite accurate, about the needs of the applicant. Is the applicant appealing primarily to the basic need to protect his family and himself from financial disaster? Does he seek ego-satisfying experiences? Is he reaching toward broader, even unchartered horizons? These are important clues to the emotional and psychological makeup of the individual. From these assumptions the interviewer makes predictions about the applicant's chances for success. Not all these assumptions and predictions are correct, of course. But they are the factors on which applicants are judged.

Skilled interviewers possess three important qualities: (1) the mental and emotional stability to make sound judgments; (2) the sensitivity to judge ability regardless of the irrelevant cues of physical appearance, speech, race, sex, geographic origin, job history, and circumstances surrounding prior job failures; and (3) the ability to understand the motivations of the applicant. These qualities give the employment interview strong potential for being a deeply satisfying human interaction. The alert applicant will play an important part in making that satisfaction a reality.

6

Where Do You Go from Here?

Evaluating Career Alternatives

One of the first reactions you may have as a sacked person is "I've had it! I'm through with the rat race! No more for me! They can have it!" And with this, you begin to withdraw from the career world you have known. You begin thinking, even dreaming, about another career where you can find happiness and satisfaction, where you can enjoy feeling respected, appreciated, and valued, even admired. That place is in your mind, in your dreams. It does not exist as you imagine it. So be prepared for something less. There are few if any utopias in the world of work. If you find one, however, don't tell anyone about it. You'll be as marked as though you had stolen the Hope diamond.

But dreams are important; fantasies play a significant role in our ability to evaluate the world, our place in it, and our desires and hopes. Daydreaming is not an unhealthy thing to do; it is O.K. In fact, when you are sacked, it may be one of the most important mental exercises you can involve yourself in. It not only provides momentary escape but allows you to test ideas within a framework of fantasy, thus releasing you from any feelings of guilt or concern. Through this process you begin to sift through alternative lifestyles. And that is what this chapter is about.

Alternative Lifestyles

Let us think of alternatives to the rat race as simply another way to lead our lives, with an entirely different set of influences and emotional reactions. Let's look at the variety of alternatives that are possible. The first thing we start with is you. Do you really want and need an alternative lifestyle, and can you sustain it for a long period of time, perhaps years? I knew an executive who decided to "drop out." He bought a tiny cottage in the mountains, near the rivers and streams in which he loved to fish. For him, it was the ideal life. His wife was not so enthusiastic, but she agreed to rough it with him if that was what he wanted. "At least," she thought, "he'll be happy. No more ulcers, late-night meetings, frantic telephone calls from the airport, and sleepless nights worrying about who is trying to cut his political throat."

For a number of months they lived in what seemed to be a mountain paradise. With the money they had saved, the stock options he had accumulated over the years, and the profits they realized on the sale of their home, they had money enough to rough it for years. But they didn't. He had given it all up after being sacked from an important executive position through the political coup of a rival corporate group. In bitterness and disillusionment, he opted for what he thought was the "good life." But wounds heal and time passes, bringing a dulling of the memory of pain. What had changed, of course, were the surroundings;

what had not changed was him. He was the same old workhorse; he still yearned for the rat race he had given up everything to escape. He still wanted the material things in life, and he began to long for creature comforts and for the signs that made him feel he was "somebody." He reentered the workforce in less than one year.

In seeking an alternative lifestyle, one of the basic prerequisites is your ability to adapt, to feel comfortable with your new lifestyle and have no regrets. That may come with time. But the question is: Are you willing to give it the time? Sometimes decisions to seek an alternative lifestyle are made too quickly after a disappointment in one's career or private life. Sometimes not enough time passes to ensure that the decision is a solid one, and worth the effort.

One of the first considerations in adopting a new lifestyle is scaling down your way of life. Being through with the rat race may mean accepting work for much less pay and giving up some things as a result. An expensive home, luxury gas guzzlers, fancy clothes, fashionable vacations, and nights at posh restaurants are obviously financial burdens to a person who chooses to "get away from it all." They are unnecessary pampering, nonessential at best to the person whose new value system cannot accommodate them.

When a person's lifestyle includes expensive tastes, that person needs to find ways to financially support them. That is when the so-called vicious circle begins. The individual is on a treadmill. I do not say these things in a negative vein; I am simply pointing out that people must be able to afford certain creature comforts, ego builders, and achievement symbols. Many people work hard in difficult and demanding jobs to support this need. I have heard many executives say that even though they detested their job and yearned for another career in a different field, they simply could not afford to give it up because they would be losing the lifestyle they wanted. It's an interesting conflict. Can an individual "scale down"? Of course, but it takes dedication and the support of a spouse if the individual is married.

A good friend of mine had a lucrative job as head of a public relations department in a national corporation. He began thinking of himself as "the corporate pimp." He gave up his $65,000-a-year job, which included a car and numerous valuable perks, to open a tiny bookstore in an oceanside town on the West Coast. He earns about $15,000 in a good year, drives an old VW, lives in a small frame house with his wife and two children, and is happier than ever before. His wife has become quite good at nature sculpture and enters many local art shows, where she has managed to sell a few pieces to help with the family's finances. He recently celebrated his sixth year in the bookstore, which, in typical fashion, he calls "The Book Pauper."

It seems to be an ideal arrangement, and for this couple it is. They had the deep dedication and motivation for the life they now live. Their children, 14 and 15 years old, had considerable problems adjusting. Neither wanted to leave the "old neighborhood," in an exclusive suburb. They did not want to leave their friends. They did not like living in the "boonies." And for the first two years they made no effort to make friends at the high school, ten miles away, to which they traveled each day in a school bus.

In time, however, the younger of the two children made friends and began working toward adjustment. The older girl cannot wait to attend college, even though she will be able to go only through a combination of funds from her father, a scholarship, and perhaps a loan—not to mention a part-time job while at school. These are, of course, obstacles she can overcome, but her life is more difficult than it might have been. Does her father feel any guilt over this? He wrote me not so long ago: "I feel badly that Chrissie dislikes our new home so much. I had hoped she would learn to see the virtues of the place. She plans to attend college, and although she will not attend in the grand style she might have had I remained in, my dream is that the experience of hard times will be good for her and help her mature. I hope that she won't think badly of me for it."

Many people who cast about for an alternative lifestyle find that it is not as easy as they thought. First of all, most want to change their career fields after devoting a number of years to a particular kind of work. They do not anticipate when they begin to seek work in some other area that prospective employers may think of them as unstable. One executive dropout told me: "Unstable? I'm as stable as anyone on this earth. Just because I don't want to be a controller any more, they think I'm unstable!" What he was reflecting, of course, was the unwillingness of employers—those who would never dream of changing careers or experimenting with more creative alternative lifestyles—to accept an individual who dared to tamper with his own life. They feared that anyone so independent would be too hard to deal with, not as cooperative as the run-of-the-mill executive.

Those who apply for work in fields other than their own quickly find out that the experience they have gained over the years doesn't do them much good in competition with other job applicants. The problem is that they often have to find a way to reapply their skills, and this may take additional education.

For example, an engineer who had worked for years in the advanced research laboratories of an electronics firm decided to change his career and become a welder. He wanted to leave the corporate zoo and work with his hands. Well, he found out that he had to return to school, enroll in a two-year program, join a union as an apprentice, and wait his turn. It was difficult for him to accept his new situation. He had 25 important patents in his name (which he had had to turn over to the company) and had written dozens of highly technical tracts on advanced electronic theory. Yet he was being beaten out of jobs by 20-year-olds. He heard that familiar, haunting line, "You're a very accomplished person but you're overqualified for our job. You wouldn't be happy here."

Sometimes people decide to embrace an alternative lifestyle within their own field. That is, they find a job at a different (usually lower) level. One production manager whom I helped place in a job decided to become a quality control inspector in a different industry. He remained in the field of production, but at a different authority and responsibility level. Some managers become consultants. Personnel people sometimes become recruiters for commercial placement agencies and executive search organizations. In such cases, there is a transfer of existing skills and of course the need to learn some newer ones, often on the job.

People are generally aware of employment opportunities in fields associated with their own. They may even know people who can be of help to them. I recall a district manager of a good chain store who, after being sacked, gained employment with a food processor that supplied some products to the chain. Although he had to learn a different angle of the business, he was able to reapply this basic knowledge. Salespeople often refocus their skills in other areas. An individual who sold real estate decides to work with a mortgage loan firm. A salesman selling consumer products sells chemicals to industry. Obviously, the individual's financial situation will change when such a shift is made. Sometimes financial deficits can be made up in a relatively short time by hard work, the reapplication of previously learned skills in the course of the new job, and a program of night school or other learning experiences.

The financial strain which may develop can be dealt with in two ways: Family members can view the financial problems as unending, or they can alter their lifestyle, scaling down their lives to match their financial means. The financial problems the family experiences may be only temporary or they may indeed be long range. If the lifestyle is not altered along with the change in income—that is, if the alternative lifestyle is resisted—the financial problems will persist. Rarely do people adopt an alternative lifestyle only to strive for the lifestyle they gave up. Starting over is not easy, particularly when people have children and lose the enthusiasm and energy they possessed in earlier years.

There is, however, an even more critical factor here. That is the possibility that personality characteristics, attitudes, and behaviors which resulted in prior job difficulties will return. So it becomes important to evaluate the causes of prior employment problems and attempt to understand their origin. It would be impossible to analyze all the behavioral, emotional, and experience-based causes of employment problems. But it is possible to discuss the roots of some common difficulties in general terms as a guide to your own evaluation process.

Analyzing Career Difficulties

In order to analyze difficulties you have had on prior jobs, you must be prepared for some pain. It's only natural. People simply cannot look at mistakes, lost opportunities, needless setbacks, and even unfairness which cost them their jobs without feeling anger, pain, disappointment, and regret. So this exercise is not an easy one. But if there is any way to dull that pain it is to remember that out of the painful experience may come understanding and insight about yourself and your needs that you have not experienced before. And the exercise will be well worth the trauma if it saves you from being vulnerable or making the same mistakes again.

It is best to take this exercise in small doses. We'll begin with the first job you ever held, working forward to the present time. This process does not have to be done at one sitting. You can work at it over a few days or weeks. Get a pad of paper and write down your thoughts about those early career days. As you begin the process, you will run through several layers of thoughts before you begin to uncover the real motivations which created changes in your career life.

Let's look at one way of describing early work experiences. We'll do it through some brief notations about a hypothetical work experience:

First job: J. R. Little and Sons, Inc.
Feelings about the job: I liked the job; felt good about it; liked the people; learned a lot; enjoyed myself. Nice people. Saved money. Got along.
Reason for leaving: To advance myself, make more money.
Reason for leaving: I got tired of the same old grind; I felt I could better myself.
Reason for leaving: They wanted to give me a big promotion; I was afraid I'd fail and didn't want to embarrass them. I lacked confidence in myself; I was afraid I couldn't be successful. They expected me to be successful.

Evaluating your own past may not come as easily as this example. But work at it. Notice the random way the words are put down, as they come to mind. You are simply groping for concepts, understandings, ideas. This isn't an exercise in sentence construction. And as you start to sift through the ideas, you'll begin to see a kind of pattern. But don't jump to conclusions. Notice in particular the three-reason ending. Typically the first reason given for leaving—the one that has probably been repeated many times to others—is not the true reason, but it is the easiest one to live with. Usually only after the second or third probe do you finally admit to yourself why you left a place you liked. You don't have to stop with a three-reason ending; you might need four or five or more. Keep fishing until you are ready to spell it out.

O.K. Let's move to the next work experience.:

Second job: Thatcher, McMurphy, and Leonard, Inc.

Feelings about the job: Not as good as the first one; good money; challenging; learning more all the time; people not as friendly; fast track. As long as I left that first job, I wanted to make it big on this one; sometimes regretted leaving; wife objected to my leaving; felt I must make it big; try hard; work hard.

Reason for leaving: Too much pressure.

Reason for leaving: Too much interference in my job from top management; too many confusing job assignments; management lacked direction.

Reason for leaving: I didn't get the proper recognition for trying hard to meet company standards; they simply didn't appreciate good effort.

Reason for leaving: The job was much too difficult to make progress in; I couldn't make it big there and make up for leaving the first job. People like me don't get ahead there; not cut out for the job.

Reason for leaving: It was clear to me I was going to fail so I got out before they sacked me.

Note that a pattern is beginning to develop in the comments about the first two jobs. It's perfectly natural to like one job over another. But the question is why—what created the problems on the job. It's obvious that the second job was more demanding; management involved itself in the work you were doing. You were not quite in control of your job and were confused. But you wanted more from that job than just success; you wanted to be vindicated for leaving the first job. In order to alleviate your guilt and prove you made the right decision, you wanted to make it big on the second job.

Still these aren't reasons for leaving. Rather, they tell you something about what you hoped to achieve on your job. When you look at the reasons for leaving, the pattern becomes clear. It's that old lack of confidence again. You assumed you could not do the job and so you escaped as you did the first time, before you were "found out." Fearful that you might fail, worried that you could not cope with failure, you resigned both times before you were sacked.

Now, let us suppose that on your third job you were sacked. Reason? Failure to aggressively pursue objectives and obtain positive results. As it turns out, this is related to the problem at the first two jobs. You begin to suspect you are a failure avoider. You would rather not pursue loftier objectives or reach for accomplishments that are difficult to achieve because you won't take some risk. Possibly you really do not want more responsibility but would prefer a job that allows you to maintain a low profile, one that is predictable and permits you a certain amount of routine. Yet you strive hard to maintain your position, feeling that hard work will give you security. Then hard work brings you challenges you really don't want, and you flee.

As mentioned before, it's impossible to analyze behavioral motives in the abstract. I am simply giving you an example of what you might uncover if you look hard enough. Notice that in my analysis I avoided value judgments of any kind; I did not indicate that an action was either good or bad. We are not attempting here to sit in judgment or to further punish prior acts. We are simply trying to put together the pieces of a complex puzzle which, despite careful and sincere analysis, may give up only a few clues to act upon. But once these few clues are unearthed, it is much easier to unearth more.

In evaluating past employment experiences, look for trends. By that I mean look for repetition, for reasons that seem to crop up again and again. One man I know who was undergoing career counseling developed a pattern of thinking of management as inept. On almost every job this individual held, he considered managers to be bunglers, unethical, lacking necessary skills, or insensitive. In a period of 11 years he held eight jobs—and lost five. Each time he either resigned because he had no faith in management's ability to steer the company on a sound path and avoid financial difficulties or was sacked because of his pessimistic attitudes about management's ability.

Upon further testing and counseling we found that this man had had similar attitudes toward his teachers in school, suspecting them of "covering up" their lack of knowledge, and thus resisted their efforts to teach. He had been asked to leave the basketball team in high school because he challenged the coach's ability and knowledge of the game. He seemed to get along more productively with female teachers than male and expressed more "respect and confidence" in the advice given to him by his mother than his father.

Although this is an extreme case, it does illustrate how patterns of behavior sometime follow us through life. Until they are isolated by what I call "reason analysis," they may go without detection. With detection, it is possible to modify your habit patterns and thus begin to alter your behavior.

Often people's employment problems are due to a feeling of alienation from their jobs, the people they work with, and their immediate supervisors. Sometimes these feelings of alienation are directed toward upper management. For example, people who tend to be absent from or late for work and who have great difficulty correcting these weaknesses are often not committed to their jobs and have not identified with the employer, the work they were hired to do, or the product and service of the company. Even excessive industrial accidents can be a latent form of alienation.

It is interesting to note that failure to attend to detail is often an indicator of potential trouble on the job. In interviewing many sacked employees, I found that initially most paid considerable attention to the details connected with their jobs. This attention began to weaken over time until they reached a point at which detail became a nuisance to them. For them, feelings of unhappiness, restlessness, and dissatisfaction followed. After that came their sacking. Understanding this pattern about themselves, they were better able to detect the early signs of disenchantment and to take steps to alter what had become almost habitual patterns. They were able to foresee trouble and either get transferred to another job or find ways of dealing with boredom and detail in order to prevent what seemed to be the next step, which was to be sacked. In short, they were able to take a hand in understanding some of the problem warnings.

For some managers, feelings of disillusionment follow what they consider defeats on the job. Highly achievement-oriented people tend to react negatively to setbacks even when such setbacks are relatively minor. Failure avoiders who wish to be free from risk situations typically venture little, gain little, and hope only to maintain the status quo in the organization. Those who require ego satisfaction on the job in the form of tangible rewards—pay increases, promotions, and more elaborate job titles—and those who need acceptance of co-workers and a lot of feedback on the job may feel alienation, hostility, conflict, and anxiety earlier in their job tenure than others.

People who have experienced a series of failures in

prior job experiences tend to anticipate failure on future jobs. Some people actually anticipate that between the third and fifth years of employment (some even between the second and fourth years) they will experience failures that will lead to their being sacked. They begin to live out a script which results in a kind of self-fulfilling prophecy. Unfortunately, many of these people never question *why* they experienced failure. They do not profit from errors because they do not identify the reasons for them.

One manager I worked with over a period of a year refused to come to grips with the attitudes he held about workers. In his judgment, every worker was a lazy, potentially disloyal person whose major interest on the job was getting the work done with the least amount of effort. This manager was convinced that workers were always trying to undermine management. It took quite a long time before he recognized that what he meant by management was himself. True, workers were trying to undermine him and were not working with him; they would seek out any opportunity to make him look bad in the eyes of management. He insisted that he was always a strong "company man" and that people simply would not give their all for the company. Again, "company" was another word for himself. When he realized that employees were reacting negatively to him because of his attitudes and behavior, he was given the key to developing a more people-oriented supervisory style. Although he understood the need, he had great difficulty convincing himself that after so many years he could actually modify his behavior.

He did, however, take several positive steps. One was to appoint an assistant who would act as liaison between him and his employees. The assistant served as a valuable buffer until he was more confident in his ability to trust his employees. He also began to analyze the causes of his mistrust. Most of the time, his employees completed their assignments when due. Still, he was mistrustful of them when he noticed them talking among themselves (he assumed it was gossip about him), being relaxed at their work (even though he tried to create tension, which he mistakenly believed spurred people to meet their deadlines), and not openly voicing concern about problems facing the department and the company. Eventually, he enrolled in several management and psychology courses that helped him learn new skills and change his supervisory style.

While it may seem to be an obvious alternative, many people do not select work which allows them to display their skills and strengths. Somehow, perhaps out of desperation and the need to find work quickly, they accept jobs which require them to function effectively in areas in which they lack strength and expertise. Any individual who does not enjoy working with people should not supervise them. People who do not enjoy the uncertainties and challenges of sales should avoid sales work. People who are not detail-minded should avoid jobs such as bookkeeping and accounting. These are obvious and very simple alternatives.

Now let's look at an example that is a bit more complex. Many people do not like to be "under the thumb" of a manager. They fear having their career and their financial situation subject to the whims of a boss. So they go into business for themselves and face all the uncertainties, financial problems, and often longer work hours just to be out from under a boss. And they are willing to put up with much more hardship as the owner of a small business than they might have had as an employee of a larger organization giving benefits, pensions, vacations, and the rest. For the self-employed, these can often become expensive luxuries. Still, to these people, there is great value and even peace and contentment in being their own boss. They feel, therefore, that they have been more than repaid for their efforts.

Evaluating Marketability

Evaluating marketability goes hand in hand with analyzing your work history and your track record as an employee. There is little question that a history of sackings can seriously damage your chances for a responsible position unless you are able to give logical and convincing explanations. Some occupations are marked by continuous sackings—for example, baseball managers and television network executives. But for the most part employees expect that a newly hired individual will do his or her best and maintain a level of performance that will make sacking unnecessary.

But, of course, sacking happens. Many people, realizing that a record of sackings will make their chances for meaningful employment slim, request to be allowed the opportunity to resign rather than be sacked. The end result is the same: they are out of work. But their work record remains unmarred.

In certain types of jobs and job levels within an organization, sackings are not necessarily damaging to the individual's career. For example, presidents of corporations who are sacked by their boards usually gain employment as the CEO of another corporation within a relatively short time. Likewise, marketing executives and advertising people who are sacked manage to come back without significant loss of prestige—at least if the sackings do not become typical of their careers. Merchandise buyers who have made wrong guesses about the public's buying mood also belong to this group.

Part of the reason such people are able to "come back" with relative ease is that they work in high-risk occupations with high visibility. Their occupations are critical to the growth and financial stability of the company. Their performance is based not only on bottom-line results but on political matters as well. These positions are often the focal point of political in-fighting. So it is not uncommon to find top executives forced out of companies due to political strife.

Political difficulties typically hamper those in upper and middle management, while "personality conflicts" commonly afflict those at lower levels in the corporate hierarchy. In any of these circumstances, the marketability of the individual is not drastically impaired. However, an individual who has led his company to financial ruin is certainly not going to find reentry into executive positions easy. Thus the question of marketabililiy after being sacked is often a matter of evaluating the circumstances that brought about the sacking and then making some predictions about how these circumstances will affect the thinking of prospective employers. The new employer must evaluate the sacked individual in terms of the contribution he can make. And so the question arises: How will the prospective employer view an applicant's track record in relation to the company's business?

If your employment record shows that you were sacked because you violated rules, performance standards, or other criteria that could have been met—and more particularly, that were within your power to meet—your record is going to be dimly viewed. You would have a better chance if the problem was politics, interpersonal relationships that went sour, and the like. The outlook is also dim if your employment record shows that you simply lacked certain expertise and that this weakness prevailed over a longer period of time than might be reasonably expected. Thus the marketability question must be answered on the basis of how you explain specific weak spots in your record and what you plan to do about them in the future. If the matter is lack of expertise, the solution may be going to night school or applying for jobs at a lower level in order to work under people who can teach you the skills you need.

In a tight employment market where there are numerous applicants for every job and where plentiful supplies of well-trained people exist, the person whose record of employment indicates weaknesses which have gone unattended over a long period will not have a good chance. Age can become a problem as well. Companies may be more willing to invest in a younger person who appears to have budding expertise, perhaps gained in recent academic studies, than to take a chance on an older person whose salary demands are higher and who still needs to learn certain skills.

Sometimes people reduce their salary requirements in order to appear more marketable, but if you are older and experienced this is not always a wise alternative. Dropping salary demands too far may signal desperation and work against you. Generally, it is better to seek a salary at roughly the same level you earned on your last job—if you are applying for a job at a comparable level. You may drop the figure slightly if you wish. Some job applicants explain a somewhat lower than expected asking price in this way: "I have confidence in my ability to produce well for this company. I want the job and I don't mind entering at a lower salary than might be expected in order to demonstrate my ability and potential. I'm confident that I can prove my work to you."

There are many pros and cons about addressing reasons for being sacked directly. Some recruiters feel that applicants who want serious consideration for employment should tell all. Others think that it is better to hedge on the subject as much as possible. If asked, "Why did you leave your last employer?" you are expected to give an answer. If you say, "I was sacked" and give no reason, you know what the next question is likely to be. "Why?" Or more subtly, "Under what circumstances were you sacked?" An indirect approach, which can be pursued even in the face of numerous follow-up questions, is this: "My immediate boss and I differed over basic work process problems and over priorities. Each of us had our own methods, and although I tried to resolve our differences and find some compromise, it was difficult. The result was that I was asked to leave." This statement is very general and ambiguous. Notice that the actual issue is never clearly addressed.

In order to evaluate their own professional status, some applicants will say: "My boss and I had roughly the same level of technical expertise, but we subscribed to quite different ethical outlooks." (Or alternatively, "different schools of thought," "different professional backgrounds," or "different points of view about the procedural requirements of the job.") They continue: "I suppose he found it easier to sack me than to try to resolve the differences, which frankly I had hoped could be accomplished."

Remember, you are the first and perhaps the only one who is going to state the case about your sacking. You can only speculate on whether the prospective employer will check with your former boss or the personnel office. Even if a reference check is made, you don't know whether the personnel office and/or your former boss will air the dirty linen. Often they won't. So take advantage of the chance to state your case first. Subsequent reference checking has to either confirm, deny, or expand on what you have said. If some of what you have said is confirmed in a reference, your statements—and the reference—will have added credibility. The important thing is not to prove who was right or wrong about your sacking but rather to show that the situation was surrounded by subjective factors and that differences of opinions are "natural" under the circumstances. This kind of fuzziness helps enhance your marketability.

I remember an individual who was fired for being tardy. In discussing the problem with a prospective employer, he explained: "Yes, I was tardy a lot. That was because at the time we had only one car. With it, I had to take my wife to work and our children to school. If I got them there too early, I was afraid they wouldn't be safe alone in those buildings. I offered to work late each day, to skip my coffeebreak, and to cut my lunch hour short to make up for it. But I was told, 'Rules are rules.' By the way, we now have a second car and my problem is solved." As I learned later, this individual did not in fact have a second car, and the problem was not solved. But his story was good enough to land him the job. Eventually he resolved the matter by arranging for a car pool for his children, for which he paid a small amount of money for gas, and his wife agreed to be driven to work a bit earlier.

At the Crossroads

Losing a job is the end of one chapter and the beginning of the next; it is both an ending and a beginning. Everyone hopes that the next phase of a career will be more successful than the last. It can be, but it won't happen by accident. Just hoping the next job will be more successful is playing a child's game of make-believe. The only thing that can make a significant difference is the manner in which you conduct yourself. Now, I fully realize that there are going to be circumstances beyond your control which may impede your progress: an unfair boss, unreasonable deadlines, poor communication, politically unstable conditions, and the like. Any of these could result in problems on the job. You then have two choices. You can stay and try to work out the problems to your own advantage. Or, if you feel you cannot survive in such an atmosphere, you can begin looking for other work.

In looking for other work, you again have several choices. You can go into business for yourself (an option we will explore below). Or you can seek employment with another company, in either your present field or a different field. If you decide to change fields and your prior experience can be reapplied, you have a definite leg up. If not, you are starting out at about the same point as people much younger than yourself. Your advantage may be prior work experience. But this has to be balanced against the needs of a prospective employer and your salary requirements. Your task at the crossroads is twofold: to analyze the causes of your being sacked and objectively determine how you might have avoided them. Don't just take your own evaluation for it. Discuss your problem with others whose opinions you respect in order to get a more objective point of view.

In evaluating your problems, you may find it helpful to review your personnel folder. You have a legal right to read what is in that folder. Get a copy and find out what is being said about you. There may be something you are not aware of. Remember too that memoranda written about you do not always find their way into your file. Often they are placed in the personal correspondence file of your boss. Thus you may not have access to all the information you need to determine what is likely to be said about you later. You might consider going to your boss, the one who is sacking you, and asking him what steps you can take to avoid such problems in the future. He may be brutally frank with you; hope that he is. He may even share some of that information in his personal file. Knowing the facts can help you evaluate your strengths and weaknesses.

Once you've isolated your problems, determine your ability and willingness to overcome them. If at that point seeking another career seems to be the only reasonable alternative, pursue that opportunity. But do so only after you've made a careful investigation and only after the wounds of your disappointment have begun to heal.

Small or Large Companies?

A few words to those who have decided, after careful analysis and adjustment of attitudes, to reenter the job market with another company rather than going into business for themselves. There is always the debate about large companies versus small. Those who have been sacked from large companies tend to want to try smaller ones, believing that they will get on better in such an environment. And vice versa. It is difficult to generalize, but we can identify certain characteristics which differentiate large from small organizations.

Let's talk about Company A and Company B. Company A is a large electronics manufacturer with a research division. It has vast markets and ever expanding research. Almost every day a new technology is discovered, a new application is found, new markets are identified. The company grows rapidly, expanding at a phenomenal rate. Turnover is high; people come and go at all levels. Salaries are high. Business pressure is equally high. A manager can boom or bust; he makes it big or he doesn't. It's what recruiters like to call a fast track. There is an air of excitement, of anticipation, of growth and profits and new worlds to conquer. And there are stresses and strains, political in-fighting for new empires which are growing within the company every day.

In such a company, if you're good you make it big; if you aren't talented, there may be a place for you; if you're marginal, you could be sacked. But even if you are talented, the politics are hot and heavy and you could get sacked through no fault of your own. You may just be a threat to someone or end up on the wrong political team. The old saying around the company is "Be kind to your fellow workers; you may end up working for them someday."

Management learns to delegate. It can't exist otherwise. Young blood is brought in and often spilled in the process, but managers mature early. They earn their wings within a short time or they wash out. The organizational hierarchy is complex, with the need to gain proper approvals for specific kinds of decisions. But managers are expected to make many decisions in the course of fulfilling their responsibilities. There are fairly clear career paths, but even in the absence of these the expansive nature of the organization gives general assurance that there will always be room at the top.

Company B is a moderate-size consumer products distributor. It may sell tomato juice today and add apple juice tomorrow, but basically the business is unchanging. Product lines increase, paperwork grows, and computer technology is added to the company. But there are internal adjustments. Business goes on as usual. Year 5 is much like year 10, and year 10 is little different from year 20 except for volume. The business is not labor intensive, so the number of employees does not increase in proportion to volume. People do not leave the organization; there is practically no turnover.

There is very little upward mobility. Jobs, if they grow, tend to expand, but there are few layers of management. The president and the chief executive officer are easily reached by telephone or in person and are on a first-name basis with most people. Salaries are not high, perhaps in the twenty-fifth percentile locally (the benefits are usually extraordinary in such companies). A strong, conservative, paternalistic attitude prevails among management. Top management believes that many years are required to learn the business, even though it is relatively simple. Small issues become major matters for management because of boredom and lack of change or new challenges. True delegation is not practiced. Managers are handed down duties which upper management either cannot or will not perform. There is a sense of security and well-being. Marginal employees know that if they can get beyond five years of service, they may well have a job for life.

There is a strong, well-known expectation of loyalty and a rather narrow code of behavior. This is partially because the company is a small, conservative organization. The company provides a relatively low-risk environment. Achievement and accomplishment are muted, and "satisfactory work" covers many levels of job performance.

Are these good or bad companies to work for? The answer depends on what you need and want in the work environment. Begin by making a list, objectively and honestly, of the ten most important elements in a job. This will help you answer the question of whether Company A or B is best for you. If no amount of money will attract you to or keep you with an organization in which there is some risk of surviving, then job security is number one on your list. If, regardless of money or security, you want the freedom to work in the style and manner that you choose, then this becomes the number one element.

Some companies encourage the high achiever, the success-oriented, materialistic individual who is willing to take risks. Some encourage the failure avoider, the nonrisk individual who would rather drive his older car than risk not having one at all. How can you tell which company is which? Sometimes reviewing growth rates will help. A company with recent, rapid growth may be type A. Very old but moderate-size companies may be type B. Sometimes the types break down by industry. For example, insurance, finance, and banking institutions often are type A. A manufacturer of consumer products may be type B.

When you visit a company during an interview, notice the ages of people who work there and the ages of those in management. This might be misleading, however, since not all conservative companies are staffed by mature managers. Reference made to the history and tradition of the company may be indicative of a type B. In such a company tradition plays an important role in influencing the course that management takes. Or the company may be attempting to fulfill an historic mandate even though the pressures of the market, competition, new technologies, and the economy may indicate otherwise. Ultimately, the decision about whether a large or small company is right for you depends on your needs, honestly addressed.

Self-Employment

Many people who are sacked from their jobs seek out opportunities for self-employment. They view self-employment as the ultimate freedom, a way to be their own boss and avoid future painful experiences such as being subjected to unfair personnel practices, having to prove themselves to an employer, knuckling under to a boss they do not respect, or working in a situation in which they feel inadequate. To many, self-employment seems to be the ultimate utopia, the one way to beat the system and survive. Most people who turn to self-employment are motivated by a desire to escape the many unhappy experiences they have had during their working lives. To be "one's own boss" is, to them, the realization of the American Dream. It represents the turning point in their lives. They view self-employment not only as a way of realizing their leadership potential as managers but as the first rung on the ladder to wealth and independence.

People who escape into self-employment sometimes view their efforts in terms of the family—that is, they include their wives and even their children, depending on the kind of business they establish. Thus they surround themselves with loved ones, those whom they trust and from whom they can expect respect and admiration. Their self-employment efforts take on the aura of a family enterprise, in which all members of the business are working together in harmony. Although there may be differences of opinion and even conflict, the overriding concern of all is personal survival. Thus conflicts are usually resolved within a reasonable period of time and without much damage to working relationships.

Most of the time, it's unwise to take the family savings and invest them in some small business simply because you need to escape. You must think these things through very thoroughly. Obtain as much professional help from bankers and investors as possible. Many people get so excited about leaving the rat race forever that they are willing to jump into almost any marginal operation, talking themselves into believing that they can make a success of it. They fantasize about their future success, the coziness of working with their wife and children. They make it all seem so logical by thinking, "Why should I work myself to death for someone else? I should be investing in my own future."

Don't rush in is my only bit of advice. And don't overlook those weaknesses which may have caused you to be sacked. Just because you've convinced yourself you should be your own boss is no reason not to strengthen yourself in every way possible. You may need every skill you can muster to survive financially. Those old habits that may have caused you trouble in the past could rise up again even though you are your own boss. Sure, you won't be sacked. But you could be ruined financially.

In spite of the statistics available and in spite of the advice given by many banking people and investment organizations, most people who turn to self-employment do so with incredible optimism. They are willing to ignore the fact that most small businesses go bankrupt within the first year. The bankruptcy rate is from 50 to 64 percent within 12 months of inaugurating a business. Most individuals escaping from the corporate scene have great faith in their ability to manage people, money, and resources. They believe that their experience working as a small cog in a multimillion-dollar operation has prepared them to run a small business. Nothing could be farther from the truth, and many people find out much too late. Let's look at the major reasons why most individuals fail in their self-employment efforts.

Underfinancing

Most people do not begin with enough financial reserve. Their optimism leads them to believe that within a relatively short time they will earn enough money to make ends meet. Underestimating the time it takes to reach the breakeven point, they usually either jump into their business venture undercapitalized or fail to obtain secondary credit sources when needed. Consequently, money runs out before they have had a chance to successfully establish their business. At that point they face the alternative of selling out or filing for bankruptcy.

Insufficient Information About the Business

Many top executives in multimillion-dollar organizations fool themselves into believing that their experience in managing a large corporate division will enable them to successfully run a small business. That is a fallacy which has brought many people to the door of bankruptcy. Running a successful corporate division is not the criterion for measuring potential success in a fledgling business operation.

Every business has its "tricks of the trade." An executive who has been in the position to hire the expertise he needs and to orchestrate the efforts of professional and technical personnel soon finds out that these experiences have nothing to do with the nitty-gritty facts, figures, and details that must be mastered in a small business. Instead of plunging their entire savings into a small business venture, such executives would do better to take a job for six months or a year as a minor clerk, if necessary, to learn something about the business they wish to own. Some managers even offer their services free of charge to owners of comparable businesses in order to learn the ins and outs.

Executives without such experience soon find that suppliers and vendors anxious to push their own products and services do not always give the fledgling business owner the best advice. In addition, competitors are often unwilling to share trade secrets with someone who has the potential of undercutting them. Most managers who turn to self-employment find that shirtsleeve management requires a new and special set of skills.

Hiring Unqualified Employees

Hiring qualified employees is one of the most critical needs of a small business, yet it is one of the weakest areas for the manager attempting to establish his own business. Managers who have spent many years in the cloistered environment of career-oriented professionals soon experience a rude awakening. On entering the retail trades, they learn, often with bitterness and disillusionment, that people earning a relatively low hourly wage do not have the employer's best interests at heart. One ex-manager, whom I knew personally, lost $7,000 in an eight-week period as a result of the dishonesty of employees who were handling his cash and inventory. Trusting, naive about the realities of operating a small retail business, my friend lacked the practical experience he needed to establish the necessary controls.

Many managers lack the practical orientation necessary to manage a small group of people in a retail store or a small service operation. Even though they have had years of management training in which they studied the theory of management, motivation, and positve reinforcement, they were unable to apply these understandings to their own retail businesses. As a result, they had to learn the hard way, often with costly consequences.

Poor Inventory Control

Many ex-managers fail in their self-employment efforts because they do not have the experience or the technical skills to effectively monitor their level of inventory. As a result, many either overstock or understock their establishments. If they overstock, they have large amounts of money needlessly tied up in merchandise which does not move. If they understock, they often miss sales and thus cut down their cash flow. Sometimes they buy merchandise which is not in demand by the consumer, and eventually it goes on sale as a loss leader.

I recall the owner of a small greeting card and gift shop who had escaped the corporate world for self-employment. The former owners of the store described the business as relatively simple, not requiring much technical information. Furthermore, they were willing to remain with him in the store for 90 days, during which time they jotted down bits and pieces of information and told him "all they knew." The result of their advice? He had to sell the store within ten months. He stocked up on items which simply did not move because he was dazzled by discounts and free merchandise offered by suppliers. He lost sales because he lacked a knowledge of merchandising and display work. All this might not have happened if he had become more knowledgeable about the fundamentals of his new business.

Underestimating the Competition

Underestimating the competition is a common failing among managers who turn to self-employment. Again, this is often a carryover from the old corporate days. The tiger who was able to eat fledglings alive, who continually experienced one success after another and kept reaching for loftier goals, suddenly finds himself out of his element. He thinks that with his background he will eat up the competition in the retail trade just as he was able to devour the competition on corporate row. He looks down the street at what appears to be a poorly or marginally managed operation and assumes that he will overtake and eventually beat the competition in a short time.

Even though such a manager may never have dealt directly with customers on a small business basis and even though he may lack firsthand experience about what goodwill in business really means, he is optimistic about his own chances of success against a long-established operation. He decides that on the basis of his prior background, his fixtures, his line of merchandise, or his own personality, he will overcome whatever competition there may be. But he fails. Why? Certainly, the problem is not one of confidence. Optimism and confidence are essential for going into business for oneself. Rather, the problem is one of *overconfidence.*

Improper Career Choice

Many ex-managers fail in their own retail business because they are simply not cut out for the work. They find it difficult to stand behind the counter waiting for customers to come in. They find it uncomfortable to bend to the whims of demanding customers who are insensitive to the needs of the business and who are not willing to hear arguments contrary to their own beliefs. In short, they have trouble believing that "the customer is always right."

Many managers find it demeaning to sweep out the store after hours, to make minor repairs within the establishment, or to even make deliveries or pick up supplies. They are simply not used to this type of life. The corporate experience has given them very different expectations. They have been catered to, feared, and respected by the people with whom they have worked. They simply telephoned someone to arrange for services. Many managers who turn to a small business attempt to purchase services which they might have otherwise provided for themselves. Unless the cash flow of their business permits, they soon find that they cannot afford to do so and therefore must learn many "do it yourself" tricks.

Some managers find it difficult to call a customer and demand their money. Others do not know how to effectively deal with vendors, trucking companies, and other suppliers of goods and services vital to the survival of their business. Many, unfortunately, do not know enough about small business accounting or the important indicators of success and failure to effectively monitor their business and identify early signs of trouble.

Managers who once had budgets that allowed them to hire expensive management consultants often invest excessive amounts of money to obtain consulting advice for their small business. They do not realize that there are government agencies which provide help to small businesses. Industry-sponsored associations also provide information about the challenges and pitfalls of self-employment. Often such managers fail to discuss their interests with current owners and bankers as well as financial consultants. They assume that they can transplant their executive skills to a small business. Rarely does transplanting work.

This is not to say that managers who have worked in corporations cannot be successful in small businesses. Quite the contrary. However, they are destined to failure unless they are able to overcome the barriers to success outlined above.

Franchise Operations

Another escape route often taken by former managers is the ownership of a franchise operation. Franchise businesses run the gamut from fast-food stores and 24-hour convenience stores to copy centers, dry-cleaning establishments, and tool-rental operations.

Several things are attractive about franchises. Many have nationally known names. In addition, the new owner need not create a new business system for his operation. He simply learns the existing accounting and marketing program, which presumably has been market-tested by the franchiser. Therefore, many new francise operators feel confident because they are not re-creating the wheel or making needless errors. They feel that with the help of the franchising organization and its established system they have a better chance of surviving than they would if they started their own business.

Most franchise operations have a business operating plan. Many require a specific store layout and provide building and merchandising facilities as part of a national program. This provides for consistent merchandising and management operations. A few franchise operations allow the franchisee to establish his business in any style he chooses so long as the franchisor's system is used. The franchisor is unconcerned about the appearance of the establishment and does not worry about standardized merchandising or servicing methods. It simply provides systems consultation.

Some franchising organizations provide elaborate training; others provide a minimal amount. The franchise organization may be highly selective in accepting franchisees, requiring prior related experience, or it may simply require sufficient investment capital. Some franchises offer continuous "field service and consultation." This means that field representatives regularly visit the franchise owner, giving advice on marketing, merchandise display, and service and even assistance with daily cash reports. Others offer the service on a regular basis—quartery, semiannually, or annually.

Some franchise operations require that the franchisee

purchase all or most of the store's merchandise from the franchisor, and all expect a return on profits. The cost to the franchisee can range from two thousand to several hundred thousand dollars, depending on the franchise. In all cases, the franchisee must give the franchise organization some percentage of gross profits, with all expenses coming out of the franchisee's share. Thus franchising organizations "get theirs" off the top, free of losses or store expenses. This figure can be as high as 50 to 75 percent, depending on the franchise organization. Franchising organizations justify this procedure on the basis of the proven success of their system, their nationally advertised name, and the fact that for a minimal investment the franchisee has the potential for an incredibly high return on investment.

Every prospective franchise owner should investigate the franchise quite thoroughly. This can be done through a number of government agencies, including the Small Business Administration and the Department of Commerce. Local and national better business bureaus should be consulted, and the financial statement of the franchising organization should be carefully reviewed by people who can understand the subtleties of annual reports. A prospective franchise owner should visit as many franchises as possible and talk with owner-operators in order to learn about franchises in general and about the specific franchise in which he is interested.

As with any business, franchise organizations are quick to advertise their successes but are reluctant to discuss the failures—and there are many, as you might expect. Simply because an individual operates a franchise with a nationally advertised name and a "proven" business and marketing system does not necessarily assure success. Franchise ownership is not a utopia, nor is it a holiday from concern. It does not relieve the individual from the responsibility of being a shirtsleeve manager. There is still the matter of hiring people, dealing with vendors, and handling the public. The basic principles of supply and demand still prevail. While the franchise organization can provide consulting support and proven methods, in the final analysis it is the franchise owner who makes or breaks the operation.

On balance, franchise operations are probably somewhat less risky than a privately owned business developed by an individual with limited expertise. The franchise organization, if it is legitimate and successful, can save the franchise owner needless and costly trial-and-error experiences in many important areas of his business, including location, traffic patterns, and the effects of competition. Still, keep in mind that franchise operations do go under. Also, the franchise operator is not entirely in business for himself. He is very much in partnership with the franchise organization and may not have total autonomy of decision making in some key areas.

A franchise which makes an above-average return on investment, which is in high demand, and which demonstrates proven results will have higher franchise fees than one which is less profitable. But this is not to say that less profitable franchises offer no opportunity to make significant profits. Again, success depends largely on individual owner expertise and the reliability and stability of the franchise organization. Only through detailed investigation and conversation with existing owners can the prospective franchise owner determine whether franchising is the route for him.

7

How to Take No
for an Answer

Anticipating Reality

Some of the most brilliant and successful people in business do not capture jobs immediately. Many wait a long time before they are accepted for a job. Job hunting is a difficult thing. If it were based solely on ability, technical know-how, and experience, it might not be quite so difficult. But it isn't. It's based in large measure on personality—how you "come across" to those who interview you—and on countless intangibles. No one can begin to guess about the various factors that affect an interviewer's perception of you. Can you know for certain all the things that instantly make you like or dislike people the first time you meet them? Sometimes your attitudes have nothing to do with them directly. It's the same way with job hunting and the job interviewer. If only there were not so much riding on every interview!

We know that the interview is made up of three facets.

The first is your ability to present yourself in a businesslike manner and to convince the prospective employer that you are the right person for the job. The second facet of the interview is the impact you make on the interviewer. You may be saying the same thing 20 other applicants said, but perhaps the interviewer likes the *way* you said it—your enthusiasm, your optimism, your warmth and sincerity. Who can say what exactly will create the best impression? If the interviewer perceives that you are reflecting some of the attitudes, mannerisms, and outlooks of others in management, this coupled with your expertise could turn the trick.

The third facet of the interview is that unknown factor—call it the Chance Dimension or the Luck Dimension. This facet includes all the little things that affect your chances of getting the job. For example, according to professional recruiters, the first two or three applicants for management jobs, whatever their qualifications, rarely get hired. The reason seems to be that during the first few interviews, interviewing managers begin to form ideas about the type of person they seek. It is not until they have tried a few people that they really settle on the personal attributes they want and the exact skills they need.

In my book *Human Behavior and Employment Interviewing* (AMACOM, 1971), I make the case that while the interviewing process is quite specific and often highly technical, the selection process itself is quite unscientific and chancy in many ways. Yet, on balance, I am often amazed what a good job professional recruiters do in matching personalities with jobs. And notice that I did not mention skills and expertise. Ultimately, the job is won not on skills but on personality coupled with skills presented in the way most acceptable to the prospective employer.

The point to remember is that the reason you fail to get a job may be tied to dimensions that not even the interviewer can define. When asked why an individual was *not* selected—assuming the reason has nothing to do with job know-how, skills, experience, or other factors in the individual's work history—recruiters will almost always mention intangible personality characteristics or even gut feel. How much of that unknown dimension is your fault? Probably very little if you've handled yourself in a conservative, well-thought-out manner. Let's be realistic. Interviewers have certain expectations about how an applicant should behave during an interview. More specifically, they have certain expectations about such behavior in relation to specific topics. Of course, these are rigid, stereotyped expectations designed somehow to make decision making easier for the recruiter. Highly qualified people may not always react in these ways, but on balance interviewers usually favor applicants who respond "on cue."

For example, interviewers expect applicants to be optimistic and enthusiastic, to feel challenged and motivated professionally when they are told the responsibilities which go with the job. When told about benefits, applicants are expected to be appreciative and to show that they value what the company offers. When told about problems, they are expected not to be depressed, befuddled, frightened, or concerned but rather to take such barriers in their stride. Interviewers expect applicants to be uncritical. They fear someone who is overly aggressive and friendly—that is, someone who does not maintain an appropriate distance. They don't really want to hear an applicant aggressively say, "I'll get that problem turned around in a hurry." Companies want problems solved painlessly and gradually. They don't want a one-man commando attack.

What I am leading up to is this: When you are rejected during an interview, the fault may not be yours. You can take full responsibility for the failures in which you know you played a primary role. *But you cannot take responsibility for intangible factors over which you have no direct control.* For the sacked individual this is a terribly important point to remember. It will help you avoid unnecessary feelings of guilt, protect your growing self-confidence, and enable you to face the next interview with optimism (an attitude which you must maintain against all adversity).

If you ignore this warning, you will damage your future chances of meaningful employment. You will be so burdened with fears, anxieties, guilt, and pessimism and so overwhelmed by feelings of failure that you will convey these negative feelings to interviewers. You may even begin to live out failure in a kind of self-fulfilling prophecy. You begin to anticipate failure and it happens. At this stage the conclusions you have reached about the direction you want your career to take hang in the balance. Even these conclusions may be tentative, pending the approval of employers. So the balance is, at best, fragile.

Obviously, you need to gear yourself for the reality of not gaining the employment opportunities you seek and for the need to look for a job over a protracted period of time. If you strike it right and gain employment earlier than expected, all the better. If not, anticpate the reality of being turned down for jobs. Anticipate the feelings of rejection, failure, guilt, even panic you will feel. Know yourself very well. Know how you react to setbacks and understand how and why you react as you do. Being prepared for emotional crisis and being ready to cope with it are your main defenses against setbacks that can undermine your confidence.

Crisis States

There are a number of emotional states you may encounter in the course of looking for a job. These states, if not identified and anticipated, can create extreme immobility among job hunters.

Once you have shaken off the confidence-shattering effects of having been sacked and have reentered the job market, setbacks often produce a feeling of bewilderment. You may be unable to muster the energy or motivation to hunt further. You feel boxed in, isolated from the active world of business and employment. These feelings can become so extreme that involuntary depression may set in, requiring psychiatric help.

Some job applicants who have experienced failure in securing work develop anxieties and fears toward particular objects or events. One manager I knew, after difficulties in the job market, developed a phobia about interviewing at the executive level—that is, at the last stage of the interview process, during which the chief executive officer or a higher management official screens the finalists. This manager's fear of failing under such circumstances caused him to clutch badly and perform poorly.

Another common response among disgruntled job applicants is antagonistic behavior toward interviewers whom they perceive as bound to decide against them as applicants. This often occurs among older management applicants who feel that even under the most desirable of employment circumstances, their age is bound to make them undesirable. Anticipating failure, they behave compulsively and sometimes voice extreme criticism of the company, its products, and its salary scale. They may even criticize the interviewer. If they deny themselves these opportunities to vent their feelings, they often feel great tension and anxiety.

Sometimes, feelings of anxiety and tension become mixed with paranoia. This is not uncommon among job applicants who have experienced repeated failures in the job market. They begin to feel suspicious of what former employers are saying about their performance and the reasons they left their jobs. They even begin to think that there is a grandiose scheme afoot to block them from working again.

Some crisis states are reflected by extreme changes in mood. People are high one hour and low the next. They get excited by the thought of a new job opportunity and respond with laughter, good humor, optimism, and the feeling that all is right with the world. Then, as the feeling of pending failure begins to take hold, their mood darkens and deep depression, tension, anxiety, and unhappiness set in. During these high (or manic) stages, an individual's appetites seem to reach insatiable proportions. During depressive states, the indivdual may turn to alcohol. These depressive cycles can be extremely harmful to the emotional and physical health of the individual. Inability to escape deep depressive moods within a reasonable period of time (and this varies with the individual from a few hours to a few days) may be a sign that professional help is required.

Waiting—the passage of time—is one of the most unnerving and anxiety-producing factors in job hunting. Time seems to always be the enemy of the unemployed. And, indeed, it may be as financial indebtedness increases, creditors display their impatience, and weeks pass into months without hope.

We think of time as our enemy because we feel we must make up for "lost time." We've been out of work, or perhaps anticipate that we soon will be. That savings account, that stock plan, or even that annuity may have to wait. We may need to hold off paying bills and so we fall further behind. At the panic stage, we think about this lost time and wonder: "Will I ever make up for it?" We think about pension plans and the years of service necessary to qualify for them. Each day spent unemployed delays the time when we can retire and reduces by that much the amount of money we could look forward to.

The key to avoiding these panicky feelings is to realize that what matters in the long run is not how rapidly we make up financial losses but how stable and long-lasting our next job will be. The security of a stable position can more than make up for temporary losses.

Sources of Crisis States

Value Systems

To the individual who has been taught that staying out of debt is essential—an honor-bound commitment—failing to pay one's bills can be highly traumatic. To the individual taught that our culture not only expects but demands that people work (harkening to the Protestant ethic), being unemployed may be tantamount to being a sinner, and the result may be overpowering guilt feelings. Yet thousands upon thousands of individuals in our society do not share these values and have no guilt feelings about unemployment. This tells us one important fact: Crisis is defined by our value systems and is internalized into feeling states. It depends on our attitudes and early learning experiences. Certain events are crises because we identify them as such.

Being turned down for a job after mustering the confidence to reenter is stress-producing without question. It is an obstacle that has been placed in your path toward a specific objective and this produces frustration. Now, remember that there are two kinds of frustration: active and passive. In active frustration not only are we blocked from achieving what we hope to accomplish but we sense some danger or threat of danger as a direct result. In passive frustration we simply do not get what we want; we fail to achieve the gratification we need. Being turned down for a job is obviously active frustration, because the prospect of continued financial loss and loss of confidence, coupled with the anxieties created by long-term unemployment, threaten our economic, physical, and emotional well-being.

Cognitive Dissonance

The theory of cognitive dissonance has direct application to the unemployed job hunter who meets repeated failure in the job market. What it means, in spite of its rather forbidding name, is this: When we are aware of two or more elements in our environment which simply do not fit together, dissonance arises—a lack of harmony with what we expect or what should be. A good example of this is the intelligent, motivated, hardworking individual with good experience who fails to find work in the job market. The individual believes that his attributes should make job finding easy. And so he thinks, "Something is wrong! Something doesn't fit together!"

For many individuals, this thought process is motivating. Why? Because most human beings cannot tolerate lack of harmony. When an individual recognizes dissonance, he sets about to make harmony; he analyzes the causes of the dissonance and makes some adjustment. If he cannot find work when he feels he should be able to, he thinks about why this is true and tries to change his approach, perhaps becoming more aggressive. He reevaluates his resume or his interview technique and may even apply for jobs with employers he might not have considered seriously before.

Cognitive dissonance often arises when an individual compares his past and his present. Many anxiety-ridden unemployed managers express deep concern about their current state of affairs in relation to the early promise they demonstrated in school or in their careers. Some talk about a successful father and their goal of repeating the father's success. Those who have come from poor families bemoan their inability to "break the chain" of the failure of fathers or other relatives now that they are unemployed and fear that this pattern of failure will follow them through life. The dissonance arises from their efforts to reverse the pattern and the results of their efforts in relation to early life experiences.

Regaining Confidence

The study of losing and regaining confidence has gone on for many years. Numerous psychologists have analyzed threats to confidence, and a number of interesting theories have evolved. Essentially all these studies, which go back to the late 1930s, indicate that the early stages of losing one's confidence are marked by depression—feelings of loss, helplessness, and isolation which simply do not go away.

When failures are experienced over and over, when there seems to be no end to setbacks, and feelings of depression and hopelessness continue, then an interesting phenomenon develops: Confidence begins to weaken. The individual begins to believe that to expect success is foolish. He anticipates failure and adopts a negative mental attitude. He also begins to feel that he is incapable of changing his circumstances. He believes that solutions are beyond him, and nothing he can do or say will ever change things. He looks about for help. Now we come to the second part of the phenomenon of loss of confidence. The individual stops problem solving completely. He finds it not only unproductive but emotionally impossible. This, of course, means that he cannot make adequate decisions. He simply exists, a child of fate, swept here and there on the wings of chance.

There are a number of practical lessons to be learned from the pattern of loss of confidence just described. If you are facing the prospect of being sacked or are already sacked and without work, take heed of the warning signals. When despair and demoralization, disappointment and anxiety set in, you may simply stop thinking. That is, you may stop problem solving because you feel helpless to turn the tide of your bad fortune.

What do you do when this happens? Well, you might begin behaving in habitual ways. That is, you do things you have always done, regardless of whether they are productive in your current situation. You behave habitually because it is the easiest way out. It requires no initiative, no confidence, no optimism, no aggressiveness, no inner drive. If you have been "pounding the pavement" in a certain way, you continue doing it even though it produces nothing. You lack the energy and the will to do anything else. Instead of getting every daily newspaper and community bulletin in town, you stick with the same old newspaper even though you aren't getting results. You call on one employment agency after another, imagining that it will come up with a job listing the other share failed to snag. You don't widen the range of companies on whom to call personally. You start thinking of yourself as being in a cubbyhole, a specific and rigid occupation.

What should you do instead in this situation? Start by thinking more abstractly and creatively about the primary emphasis of your job. Sit down and list all the attributes, aptitudes, important and unimportant skills you have utilized on jobs in the past. Then, begin to rearrange these skills like pieces in a puzzle to form ideas about a new job for you. Thus an accountant who deals with detail and numbers may begin to think of himself as everything from an inventory control analyst to a quality control inspector; he begins to think of ways to use his detail orientation if he were to change occupations—for example, into programming or systems work. An individual who has spent years "selling" management on new ideas and who works well with people begins to see that those qualities are essential for sales work and may look for a sales trainee position. People who have worked with company benefits often find their way into group insurance sales. People who have spent time in purchasing and receiving functions begin to picture themselves in traffic and even dispatching.

In short, rather than following the same old pattern, try to be original and creative. Let's define what originality means. Originality is an uncommon response to a common problem; it's something different, a new way of approaching the old. For all practical purposes, originality carries with it some risk. The risk, of course, is that of failing. But if old methods are failing, newer approaches, at their worst, can't do much harm. And new approaches carry new hope.

Your personality will play a part in how original you can be without changing some basic behavior patterns. Most people who display originality are open, willing to experiment, lack defensiveness, are willing to take some risks, and are not likely to go to pieces if they experience failure. Intelligence alone is no guarantee of originality. The original thinker usually hesitates to draw rapid conclusions, preferring instead to think, observe, and always *try*. He does not assume that something is doomed to failure; he reserves such judgments and continually asks, "Why not?" He never gives in to the anticipation of failure or of looking foolish.

Can you learn to be more original? Of course. Many studies done by psychologists show that this is possible. Start on a small scale. Try to "brainstorm." That is, think in "blue sky" terms without fear of punishment or ridicule. Plan a meal you'd love to eat. Think of all the things you could include. Have fun with it. Think of a trip you'd like to take. Imagine the places you'd like to go if you could afford any dream trip in the world. Then make a game of it. Think of all the places you could go that travel agencies do not have tours for! Think of twelve ways to change your front yard without using grass!

Do you know what you are doing? You are coming up with alternatives. You're problem solving! You're thinking!

A philosophy professor I had once challenged us with this question: "Describe a form of existence that has no shape, density, volume, or visual or audible qualities, that cannot be touched or smelled and cannot be heard or seen?" We were forced to extend our imagination beyond our own experience of reality. You needn't go quite that far. But you could go as far as your local library and get a copy of the *Dictionary of Occupational Titles*. You'll be amazed at how many occupations are included. Try to define all the ones that have skill requirements you can meet now or could meet in a short time with a little training.

You are going to find the job you want and need. It's a matter of time. The time can be shortened by the positive, productive, original, and aggressive steps you take at this juncture of the road. Your mental attitude will have more to do with your ability to gain a job than almost anything else. As I have pointed out, there is no substitute for lack of skill. You can't get a job you can't perform regardless of your positive mental attitude. But given the skills, confidence and optimism about the future are your best allies.

If you think that being turned down for jobs is depressing, think back to that moment when you found out you were sacked! Most people come a long way emotionally from that point in their lives to the point at which they can face the job market again and take the temporary setbacks without going off the deep end. Still, the toughest task ahead may not be getting that next job but keeping it once you've got it! That is where the real payoff of all your self-analysis will come. That is where you'll know you've overcome those obstacles that created your sacking in the first place—if, in fact, the obstacles were of your own making.

You'll never find that perfect job. It doesn't exist. There will always be politics, unfairness, tasks you can't fully perform, and mistakes you'll make for no other reason than that you are human. Don't worry about those things. They do not belong to any one industry; they have nothing to do with the size of a company or its products or services. They simply arise wherever people work together. Your task is to worry about yourself—to be aware of and sensitive to yourself and your needs, your strengths and your weaknesses, your fears, your outlook on life, and the way you perceive the future and your place in it. Your value as an individual is the same now as when you were employed. Nothing has changed that. With the proper analysis and concern for yourself as an employee, your worth may very well increase.

Regardless of the environment in which you find yourself, in spite of the outside events which affect your life, you bear responsibility for your actions and for your successes and failures. Once you accept that responsibility, once you embrace it willingly and enthusiastically, you will have matured and reached a point of self-fulfillment beyond your farthest expectations. And what is so beautiful is that it is within your own power to achieve. As you gradually move toward that realization, your inner strength and respect for yourself will rise proportionately. Accept the failures as your own and learn from them. And claim the successes you will rightfully deserve.

8

Postscript:
Women and Minorities

There are special problems confronting women and minority workers who have been sacked. Many laws exist today to protect minorities, who traditionally have had trouble entering the job market at productive levels. With the equal employment opportunity legislation, which prohibits discriminatory practices or policies, attention has been focused on the rights of minority applicants for jobs. This is not to say that these important pieces of legislation have eliminated discriminatory practices from the job scene. If this were true, our nation would not still be squandering so much of its precious human resources. But conditions today are better than they have ever been before, though they are far from what they should be.

Dealing with Discrimination

Women and minorities who have had so much difficulty securing meaningful work for themselves, who have overcome considerable barriers to achieve success in the job market, may view their sacking in a somewhat different light than those who have not faced the sting of discrimination. Often minority people feel a sense of betrayal, of disillusionment. They feel that their deepest mistrust of management has been confirmed, that all along they have been fooled into believing that, in fact, they had a chance at higher-level achievement.

Minority people who are sacked always are concerned about whether their sacking resulted from their minority status and whether they were being judged by the same standards as others. As I have mentioned, looking for precedents within the company is probably the best way to determine if discrimination in fact exists. Simply stated, if others are late too, but you are reprimanded and they are not, that may be a sign of bias. If the mistakes of others are overlooked but you are held strictly accountable, that may be a further sign of bias.

When economic conditions force a company to lay off employees, minorities and women are often among the first to go. This may not be discrimination. Keep in mind that minorities and women have entered the job market in large numbers only within the past five to ten years, often working for companies that previously found ways to avoid hiring them. Most layoffs begin with those having the shortest service or those working at lower hierarchical levels in the organization. Also, many minorities are in unskilled and semiskilled jobs, some just entering positions which have the prospect of being meaningful. Here again, the pattern of layoffs can be analyzed. If, for example, white employees with comparable service have a lower percentage of layoffs than minorities, a discriminatory pattern may exist.

When patterns of discrimination are discovered, there are several alternatives available. One is to discuss the matter with employers and union representatives and attempt to resolve inequities. Another step is to seek relief through government agencies, such as the Equal Employment Opportunity Commission and the Fair Employment Practices Commission. Minority employees can also ask local activist groups to intervene with employers and attempt to resolve unfair practices without involving the government bureaucracy.

Reentering the Job Market

In evaluating job applicants, the only clues the prospective employer has to go on are his emotional reactions to the applicant during job interviews, letters of reference, if any, and the general pattern of employment. The pattern includes such factors as job titles, the kind of work performed, and whether such work progressively advanced or remained at the same level over a number of years. Another measure might be salary. Has it progressed gradually or has it remained level or even decreased? Longevity on jobs is another indicator. If a person has hopped here and there, either being sacked or resigning but never being laid off, it may indicate instability, unhappiness with the type of work performed, or difficulty keeping jobs.

These factors make employers concerned about the ability or willingness of the applicant to remain on the job if hired. If the individual is a minority applicant, the employment pattern may be judged as reinforcing biases about a particular race or it may be viewed as an exception if the record is better than expected. A marginal or questionable work record added to the problems of discrimination can create barriers to being employed.

Many professional recruiters note that conveying mistrust, displaying a clear unwillingness to accept the prospective employer on faith, and holding back loyalty and commitment to the job are real problems which confront the minority applicant. Again, this is not a suggestion of blame; it is merely a recital of circumstances which both employer and applicant need to recognize. There is, of course, suspicion about minorities on the part of employers, and every minority applicant should understand the basis for this suspicion.

We have moved past the time when employers worried that their employees would refuse to work for a company that hired racial minorities. Employers often used that excuse for not hiring minority workers, as well as the excuse that customers or suppliers would object and create unnecessary business problems. Today employers are expressing a somewhat different concern, but it points to the same result: restricting the employment and advancement of minority people.

The new concern is that, once in the organization, minority employees will become a troublesome element, always pushing for rights, making demands of management not only to further themselves but others as well. With the growing women's movement, which has crossed racial lines, an entirely new dimension has been added— that of women's rights in the business world. From time to time the courts have handed down startling decisions which cost some companies millions of dollars in back pay or damages to women and minority employees as a result of class-action suits. Thus the threat of minority unrest and agitation is real to many employers.

How should minority applicants confront the special problems they face? If you are a minority member, follow the guidelines for interviewing established in Chapter 5. Be aware of the factors creating employer mistrust and address them openly and directly. Do not charge discrimination on the part of a past employer, because most prospective employers will view such a statement as covering up for your own weaknesses and as an indication of what they might expect from you if hired. It is, of course, your decision to make. You can accuse another employer of discrimination and even state that you have taken legal action as a show of your independence and resolution. Employers cannot legally deny you a job for these reasons. But as you well know, they don't need such reasons not to hire you. They can find dozens more that are perfectly legal. My advice is not to make an issue of your sacking during an interview, even if you were unfairly treated. State your case clearly and objectively and in sufficient detail and leave it at that.

Although I don't usually advocate personal references, minority people may find them useful, especially if they have very limited work experience or inconsistent patterns of employment. In such a case, the prospective employer has few clues to the capabilities, interests, and employment value of the applicant. Personal references, while not ideal, help close this gap, providing additional insight into the applicant's abilities and character.

The value of personal references often depends on who is writing the letter. Suppose the pastor of a church writes a letter indicating your dedication, hard work, and attention to detail during many fund-raising drives. Suppose the local high school principal writes a letter indicating what a sound leader and effective intermediary you were for the PTA in parent-teacher conferences. Suppose a well-known national society writes a letter indicating that you have held a number of administrative offices and performed admirably in all of them. Such letters say something about you as an individual, and they comment on your integrity, your ability, and your character. They have a positive influence and cannot be wholly ignored. In the absence of reference information on your performance on previous jobs, such letters can be of value and significantly aid your chances for employment.

Index

adjustive reaction(s)
  apathy as, 21
  compensation as, 20
  conversion as, 20–21
  displacement behavior as, 22
  fantasy as, 22–23
  fixation as, 21
  projection as, 22
  rationalization as, 22
  reaction formation as, 22
  regression as, 22
  repressive behavior as, 21–22
advertisements, help-wanted
  reading, correctly, 77–79
  salary requirements in, 71–72
age
  antagonistic behavior due to, 158
  of employees, as indication of company attitude, 143–144
  marketability and, 137
  on resume, 81–82
aggressive behavior, as response to job loss, 15
alienation, as employment difficulty, 131–132

anxiety, 17
  causing, as defensive technique, 52–54
  confronting, 5–6
  coping with, 3–5
  frustration and, distinction between, 1–2
  high vs. low, 6–7
  in interviews, 93–94, 119
  as motivator, 7–8
apathy, 21
automobile
  as collateral, 31
  as expense, 30

behavior patterns, as clue to employment difficulties, 131

career
  alternatives, evaluating, 121–122
  choice, improper, in self-employment, 149–150
  difficulties, analyzing, 127–135
  franchise operation as, 150–153
  goals, 3